Race Week – The Final 7 Days to Your Best Triathlon

Race Week –
The Final 7 Days
to Your Best Triathlon

by Paul Regensburg, LifeSport Coaching
"The Official Coaches of Ironman"

Meyer & Meyer Sport

IRONMAN® is a registered trademark of World Triathlon Corporation

British Library Cataloguing in Publication Data
A catalogue record for this book is available from the British Library

Paul Regensburg, Race Week – The Final 7 Days to Your Best Triathlon
Maidenhead: Meyer & Meyer Sport (UK) Ltd., 2010
ISBN 978-1-84126-117-1

© 2010 by Meyer & Meyer Sport (UK) Ltd.
Aachen, Adelaide, Auckland, Budapest, Cape Town, Graz, Indianapolis,
Maidenhead, New York, Olten (CH), Singapore, Toronto
Member of the World
Sport Publishers' Association (WSPA)
www.w-s-p-a.org
Printed and bound by: B.O.S.S Druck und Medien GmbH, Germany
ISBN 978-1-84126-117-1
E-Mail: info@m-m-sports.com
www.m-m-sports.com

Contents

INTRODUCTION

You've trained the best you could, you've committed time and money, you've altered your diet to one of Power Bars, sports drinks, and gels – and now you've come to the last week before your race. Congratulations on making it this far, you have just a little bit farther to go. No matter what your ability, triathlons are a challenge – a challenge to be embraced, and although you cannot really change your fitness level at this point, the final week can make or break you race.

The week before your race will inevitably be a bit frantic, but this can be easily tamed with a little bit of help. Having the proper tools, like those found in this book, will help to smooth out your week and give the confidence needed to realize your goals – goals that have been months in the making. This book is designed to guide you, the athlete, through your last week of training, and to cover all the last minute questions and concerns that will come up during this time. It will take you through everything from final workouts, to dealing with the environment, to mental preparation, and will work to sharpen your skills and knowledge about training, racing, nutrition, and equipment.

Being a triathlete is far from easy and I'm sure you've come to realize this by now. But what you'll also know is that there's nothing like the feeling of moving well across the water in the swim, slicing through the air on the bike, and your feet floating above the ground on a run. There's nothing quite like setting a goal and seeing it through, and there's nothing quite as rewarding and exhilarating as crossing that finish line. This book will help you get there feeling your best and proud of your accomplishment.

Let's make this a great week!

© Dan Smith

1 Setting up for Success

PREPARATION

Strong preparation is essential to having a good race experience, and most athletes will have a bad race experience to back this theory up. Preparation is the backbone to any successful race and there are still a lot of meaningful ways to prepare during race week that can influence your race positively.

DO YOUR RESEARCH

Although pre-race meetings will cover most of the technical aspects of the race and course, talking with athletes who have completed the race before can be very helpful in learning specific race features that may not be addressed otherwise. Go online and research the area, read some forums, check the forecast, and explore accommodation options. Find out where the training venues are and if there are any specific equipment requirements. When you really do your homework, there is a much better chance for success.

MANAGE YOUR TIME

In the days leading up to your race it's going to seem like there is an unlimited number of things to do. Create a schedule and task list for your last week including all workouts, appointments, packing time, bike servicing, and other "to do" items. Give yourself ample time for these tasks and don't forget to include time for sleep, rest, and proper nutrition.

FAMILIARIZE YOURSELF WITH THE COURSE

Almost all races will provide a course map in their race package, and many will also have the map available online. Take some time to read through the course description and make note of aid station locations, terrain, elevation changes, and technical sections. Part of your responsibility as a triathlete is to know the course – train on the course if possible, well in advance of the race. If you can only see the course on race week, then it is a good idea to get to the course early and use it for your race preparation workouts. Swim on the course at the same time your race starts on race day to check out the conditions. Ride on the bike course, or at least sections of it, and if time does not allow, you may want to drive it (although it does feel much different in a car). A good way to see the run course is to ride it on your bike if you are saving your legs for race day or run shorter sections to get a feel.

ATTEND THE PRE-RACE MEETING

Triathlon events will often hold a pre-race meeting the day before a race. Although these meetings seem like another task, it is not a bad idea to attend for a quick review or to ask the race director any questions that may be lingering. It also offers the opportunity to meet with people you know and to discuss the race. Some meetings are painless and only last around 15 minutes, while others can be over an hour. If getting to a meeting is going to add unnecessary stress to your plate, ask a buddy to fill you in on items that may differ from the pre-race information that you were given.

© fotolia, Brian Jackson

ACCOMMODATION

There are many factors to consider when it comes to choosing accommodation. To start, check out the official race hotel or consult a travel agent, travel guide and check online sites for recommendations. Many race websites will list good accommodation options that are close to the race venue. Once you've decided on how much you want to spend, you should consider whether you'd like to be near the race venue or farther away – each has pros and cons.

NEAR THE RACE SITE

Pros

- Race venue is generally within walking distance.

- More access to conveniences of the city (restaurants, bike shops, etc.).

- Host hotel is accustomed to having athletes and often will offer things like bike storage, race briefings, info centers, and carb-rich meals).

- Closer to race expo where you can pick up your registration package and see exhibitors.

- More likely to run into friends, people you know, and other racers.

Cons
- Race tension in the air with all athletes in same areas.

- City congestion – difficult to run or ride because of the central, busy location.

- Can be expensive.

- Accommodation is often small and won't offer kitchen facilities.

AWAY FROM RACE SITE

Pros
- More peaceful and relaxing—away from hype of the race.

- More options and amenities are available—better for family.

- Often more rural and beautiful, good for training.

- Likelihood of getting a condo at a cheap price is better than close to venue.

Cons
- Travel time to get to race functions can be long. You will have to wake up early on race morning to allow time to get to site.

- Can take away from the relaxing benefits, as you have to be on the road for longer periods of time.

CONDO VS. HOTEL

Some athletes prefer to rent a condo for the length of their stay, and although it is more expensive than a hotel, it is highly recommended. A condo is more home-like and comfortable – you get your own room and kitchen, and have much more space for your bike and equipment. If cost is an issue, look into sharing a condo with another couple. Websites such as VRBO.com (Vacation Rentals by Owner) can help you find an available condo in your race area with just a click.

TRAVEL

Going to places you haven't been before can be exhilarating. Getting there, on the other hand, can be quite the ordeal. It's no secret that traveling to a race venue is tiresome and uncomfortable, but there are ways to work around this. Follow these simple travel tips to add some ease to your journey.

FLYING

DO bring your running and cycling shoes, racing suit, and goggles on flight as carry on. This way, if your luggage goes missing you'll have what is essential.

DO choose a seat toward the front of the plane. Oxygen is discharged into the cabin from a source at the front of the plane.

DO keep hydrating with electrolyte throughout travel.

DO travel in comfortable clothes and consider compression socks for leg circulation.

DO pay an extra fee for an exit row. This is a good investment as it offers more leg space.

DON'T book a flight with a long layover. Even if it is a bit more expensive, it's better to pay the price than get stuck at the airport for five hours.

DON'T sit in an aisle seat if you plan on getting some shut eye. Get a window seat if possible.

DON'T get sick. Bring hand sanitizer and wash hands frequently to reduce the risk of picking up harmful germs.

DRIVING

DO drive if the venue is close to home. It will be cheaper and easier to get around once at the race location, and car-pooling can help cut down on the price of gas.

DO give yourself some time to rest once you arrive.

© Dan Smith

DON'T drive for extended periods. If the ride is long, go with someone you can share driving duties with. If the drive will be over five hours you should think about flying.

BIKE BOXES

There are a few options available when it comes to packing your bike for travel.

1. Hire a company affiliated with the race (Ironman uses TriBike Transport), and drop off your bike at a partner bike shop a few days before event. The company will ship your bike to a bike shop in race city where it will be reassembled and ready to go when you arrive.

2. Use a courier to ship your bike (UPS, FedEx). If possible ship to a local bike shop where they will reassemble it for a fee.

3. Travel with bike – check with baggage.

Bike boxes can get expensive to bring on flights if you are charged fees for weight. It's best to research the airline and their policy on bike boxes before committing to a flight, as the costs for seemingly cheap flights can add up fast. Some airlines will charge a lot while others will charge next to nothing. If traveling by plane, consider using a soft case. Although they may not protect quite as well as the hard case, they are lighter, smaller and easier to manage – and will sometimes not be charged the extra bike fee!

PACKING A BIKE BOX

Fretting the ordeal of dismantling your bike and wrestling it into a bike case? Packing a bike can actually be accomplished with relative ease if you have the proper tools, know the right sequencing, and have had some practice. Become a master bike packer by following these steps:

Step One: Remove Pedals
Tools: 15 mm pedal wrench or 6 or 8 mm hex wrench (Allen key), depending on pedal type.

Start on the left side of your bike and turn crank to the forward horizontal position. Set the pedal wrench onto the spindle of pedal so the handle is pointed towards the rear wheel. Push the handle down, turning clockwise, to prod spindle lock from crank. Keep turning until pedal is removed.

Go to the right side (where chain rings are) and perform the same procedure as on left side, but this time turning the wrench counter-clockwise. If pedals are tightened down too hard against the crank, use a rubber mallet to gently tap the handle of the wrench.

Step Two: Remove Handlebar
Tools: 4 or 5mm Allen key (in rare cases a 6mm one), tape.

If you have a speedometer, remove it first, and tape it to your frame or fork. Your handlebar is attached to a stem that is secured to the fork's steering tube. The handlebar stem has a front plate which holds the handlebar in place with either two or four holding bolts. Remove all bolts and take the handlebar off the stem and let it hang loose on the cables. Reinstall the top plate onto the bar stem, so you do not lose any of the small parts.

Step Three: Remove Seat
Tools: 4 or 5mm Allen key

Open up the bolt on the seat post holding clamp by turning it counter-clockwise, only to the point that you can pull out your seat post. Remove the seat (and seat post) from the seat tube.

Step Four: Remove Wheels
Tools: Small Bag

Start on front wheel and open up the brake calipers by moving the quick release lever upwards so they are farther away from rim. Open the wheel holding quick release lever, hold lever in hand, and turn the opposite side adjuster nut counter-clockwise until the wheel falls out freely. Pull out the skewer and thread the adjuster nut back on. For the back wheel, shift into the smallest cog on cassette and follow the same sequence as front wheel, starting with brake calipers. Remove the skewer and lift up bike with left hand. Apply some force on tire with your right palm until wheel pops out of frame. Lift the chain over the rear cog so the wheel can be removed. Place pedals and skewers together in a small bag.

Step Five: Placing Frame and Loose Parts in Traveling Case
Tools: Frame and fork saver, Rag, Zip ties

First insert frame and fork savers into the dropouts. Put your bike on the ground with the drive train facing up. Wrap your chain stay with a rag before you attach your derailleur to the frame. Pull the derailleur cage to the farthermost position towards the center of the frame. Tie the cage with a zip tie to the frame so derailleur won't hit the side of the box and get damaged.

Place your bike in the box. Turn the fork to the right so the brake on the fork is facing you. Set the handle bar down between the fork and down tube so the top of bar is facing you. Adjust your bike so that it sits nicely in the box and is not forced. Secure frame with the supplied straps keeping it in the center of the box. Place a layer of foam on top of the frame.

Step Six: Place Wheels in Case
Tools: Rag or cloth

Let the air out of the tires leaving a maximum of 30 PSI for air travel. Place your front wheel over top of the front section of the frame (over the handlebar). Wrap the cassette on the rear wheel with a rag, and place the wheel with the cassette facing up, close to the rear end of the frame. Wrap your seat in a rag and place in case, away from sharp edges. Do not forget your bag with small parts. Cover your wheels with foam. Secure lid.

TIME ZONES

The best way to become accustomed to a new time zone is to simulate in advance. If you plan to race in a city that is three time zones ahead, prepare by waking up 3 hours early the week before the race. It is always best to fall into a normal pattern as soon as possible, so the further the time zone, the earlier you can arrive, the better.

Rule of Thumb: one day is needed per time zone to adjust. Example: If you live in Vancouver and will be racing at Ironman UK in Bolton, England (8 hour difference), arrive 8 days before the race.

FAMILY

For athletes with a family, day to day life can become quite the balancing act. Training and racing can take a lot of time and energy, and families will often bear the brunt of this hectic lifestyle. Traveling to a race with your family can turn into a great vacation, but it can also add stress to an already stressful weekend. It's important to decide whether it is better for your family to travel with you to an event or to join you later, or whether to come at all. Consider the following strategies with the family...

CHOOSE THE RIGHT PLACE TO RACE

Choose a race that is in a location that will be enjoyable for everyone, and search for fun activities that you can do with your family before or, preferably after your race. When choosing accommodation, pick a place that is family orientated (pool, cable, movies, etc.)

PREPARE YOUR FAMILY

Plan ahead and pack all the little odds and ends that will make everyone more comfortable. Make sure to discuss your expectations with your loved ones and let them know your schedule and obligations so there will be no surprises. It can also be helpful to create a "family package" that includes course maps and information, your number, and anything else that will help them feel more a part of the experience.

© fotolia, Kzenon

OCCUPY YOUR FAMILY

While you are kept extremely busy throughout the day, your family most likely won't be. Overcoming race day boredom can be a challenge. If you are doing a long race, consider having your family there to see you start, going off to do something fun, and returning later. It can also be beneficial to encourage family members to become volunteers. This way everyone has something to do and can be part of the excitement.

GIVE YOURSELF THE TIME YOU NEED

Make a solid commitment – before the race is your time and after the race is family time. Before heading out to take part in family activities, take all the time you need to relax and recover. It's understandable that you'll want to spend time with your loved ones as soon as possible, but the day will be more enjoyable for everyone if you take the time to recuperate. Take pleasure in the fact that you've just completed a triathlon and are surrounded by the ones you love. Enjoy the rest of your time!

© ASI Photos

2 Your Equipment and Gear

Entering your race week you should be well-equipped and well-practiced on that equipment. Every piece of equipment you plan on using during your race should be equipment that you've trained with unless alterations are absolutely necessary. Changing equipment in the week before a race could hurt you and the outcome of your race, so stick with what you know and what is proven to work!

Review and check your equipment before you travel, at the race location, and again in the morning of the race. This includes a self bike check (brake pads, seat, handle bars, tire pressure), your shoes, clothing, special needs bag, and even your nutrition. Avoid the temptation to purchase and try new equipment and clothing for the race – race expos can be very tempting. As you get closer to the race there can still be a number of equipment decisions to make based on the specific conditions that the race presents.

SWIMMING EQUIPMENT

RACING SUIT

A one-piece triathlon suit may be the most comfortable and effective but you may opt for a two-piece suit in hotter conditions or personal preference. Whether you are swimming in a wetsuit or not can make a difference in what you wear underneath. If wetsuits are allowed you can wear pretty much anything you like underneath because it will not pick up drag in the water and dry quickly once you are on the bike. If wetsuits are not allowed, be sure to wear a suit that is made for swimming – non-absorbent, smooth materials (i.e. – no pockets). If you are wearing a traditional swimsuit and plan to bike with only this, be sure to apply lots of lube to your legs to avoid chafing. In longer-distance races, it is quite acceptable to change from your swim gear into dry cycling/run gear to be comfortable for the rest of the day.

WETSUIT

Wetsuits are ideal for colder, open water courses, and should be worn whenever allowed. A wetsuit offers warmth and buoyancy which will result in faster swimming speed. Wetsuits come in full or sleeveless options. Full suits cover most of the body, giving the best protection against the cold and are generally faster because there is more neoprene in contact with the water for buoyancy. Sleeveless suits are more comfortable and allow for better arm motion when swimming but can also let more water into the suit. Try to find a full suit that is as tight as possible in the body but still allows for good arm mobility.

© Fotolia

WETSUIT TIPS

Putting Suit on

- Lube your forearms and shins with a lube stick, Vaseline, or cooking spray for quick removal.

- Use plastic bags over your feet and hands to slide easily through the legs and arms of wetsuit.

- Roll wetsuit over so you pull up the neoprene by the inside to avoid getting fingernail tears on the outside.

- Pull up high in the crotch before pulling over torso and inserting arms (using same method of pulling up rolled up neoprene from the inside).

- When arms are inserted pull up very high on shoulders to give slack.

- Wetsuit can be very tight as long as the arms can move freely in circles.

- Secure zipper at top, lube back of neck liberally.

- Some athletes will cut bottom of legs a bit shorter to allow the suit to come off easier with not getting caught on ankles.

Taking Suit off

- When racing and you are exiting the swim – don't attempt to remove wetsuit until you are clear of the water and your feet are on dry ground.

- First, don't remove your swim cap and move your goggles up onto your forehead (don't remove) so your hands can be free to remove suit.

- Unzip suit and take off to your hips leaving the suit on from your waist down as you run to T1.

- Once in transition, remove cap and goggles, pull wetsuit down over hips to knees and then lift one knee high at a time to pull suit off, step on the suit with the other foot to hold it in place while the knee comes up until the suit falls off.

© Dan Smith

LUBE

Lubrication is important to prevent chafing, rashes, and makes wet suit entry and exit much easier. It often comes in a deodorant style stick, and won't take up much space when packing. Some athletes will use canned cooking spray to lube their skin instead of a lube stick or Vaseline to keep their hands dry and free of residue.

GOGGLES

Buy high quality goggles – this is a small investment that will make for a much better swim. Race with newer goggles but make sure that it is a model that you are accustomed to and you've had a few swims to break them in. Newer goggles will be clearer and less likely to fog. Have a pair of tinted goggles ready to go for swim courses that have a rising or low sun on the horizon. Another good trick is to put your swim cap on over top of your goggle straps so they are not exposed to the possibility of being pulled or slipping when on the outside.

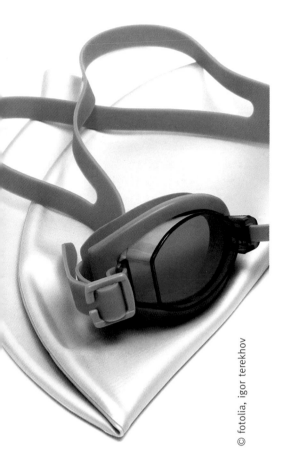

© fotolia, igor terekhov

SWIM CAP

Normally you will get your race swim cap from the race organizers so you do not have a choice in what type your wear. Swim caps are pretty standard so this should not be an issue but if it is a cold swim you can wear your own swim cap underneath the race cap – "double capping" – for extra warmth.

EAR PLUGS

If you are susceptible to ear infections, ear plugs can help minimize the amount of water that enters your ears. Ear plugs come in different varieties but for swimming the moldable wax plugs provide a very good seal. This is also a sure fire method of reducing or eliminating motion sickness in the water as well.

SUNSCREEN

Sunscreen should always be applied in warm to hot races. The best time to apply is in the morning before the swim and then as the race goes on depending upon the length of the race. The skin is the largest organ in the human body and if burned, the sweat gland function promoting dehydration will be hindered. Burned skin can't regulate temperature as well as normal skin, therefore the body's ability to cool itself is inhibited. Look for sport sun screens that allow the skin to breathe with good SPF's that are easy to apply. Don't miss any spots – especially on your back around the edges of your racing suit.

TOWEL

Choose a bright, recognizable towel that you can lay in your transition area and spot easily upon exiting the water.

BIKING EQUIPMENT

HELMET

Check your helmet on race week to ensure the straps are comfortable and provide a snug fit. The chin strap should not be too loose under your chin or the officials may make you tighten it up before you leave transition, which is not an easy operation when you are in the middle of a race. Cold hands can also make it difficult to connect the clasp on the chin strap. Before the race make sure that the clasp is connecting well and practice this a few times.

Some athletes will also make the decision on the race week between an aero versus a traditional helmet. An aero helmet is faster but will also be hotter and can provide some wind resistance if there are crosswinds.

BIKE SHORTS

Some athletes may want to wear traditional bike shorts for the cycling segment of the triathlon particularly if it is an Ironman distance race. This can be done by wearing the cycling shorts underneath the wetsuit (although the chamois can absorb a lot of water and be uncomfortable) or changing after the swim. Either scenario will most likely be slower but if sheer speed is not your goal then the comfort may be worth it.

BIKE SHOES

If you cycle in bare feet, lube your shoes where your feet may rub continuously to prevent blisters and cuts. You may want to also glue the insoles down to the bottom of the shoe so they do not bunch up when you slide your feet quickly into the shoes in race conditions.

JERSEY/JACKET

In most races you will not need a jersey for the bike and your swimsuit will suffice. If you are in a race where you are performing a full clothing change, or the weather is cool, you can slip on a jersey and light tight-fitting jacket to stay warm.

CYCLE GLOVES

There is a lot of pressure put on your palms and hands while riding, so padded riding gloves will make things a lot more comfortable for you during the bike leg of the race. Cycle gloves will also help in the event of a crash, as it is natural instinct to use hands to break a fall.

ANTI-CHAFE FOR BIKE/RUN

Applying or reapplying anti-chafe while on the bike (Vaseline, Chamois Butter, Body Glide, etc.) directly on the skin will reduce any rubbing that may result from a long time on the saddle. This will also come in handy during the run – especially under the armpits and on the nipples.

SUNGLASSES

You get what you pay for when purchasing sunglasses for triathlon. In addition to looking cool, shades should be durable, comfortable and have good quality lenses that will shield eyes from UV rays. Sunglasses will also provide protection from debris flying up from the road and will ease strain on the eyes and face, which conserves energy.

CO_2/PUMP

Experienced triathletes prefer to use CO_2 inflators to fill up their tires during a race, as they work to save weight and time. Carry at least 2 CO_2 cartridges and practice using them well in advance of the race. CO_2 leaks more rapidly than air, however, and if you are new to using CO_2, or have fears of it malfunctioning, a frame mounted pump is always a fail-safe method for back-up.

BOTTLES/HYDRATING SYSTEMS

The amount of bottles attached to your bike is up to you. Many riders will have a cage on both of their down tubes, but for longer distance races where more hydration is necessary, riders will attach a system that carries two bottles on the back of their bike, as well as a bottle between their aero bars. Practice using each system before the race.

FLAT KIT

Seat bags on the back of your bike seat and seat post are a good way to carry spare tubes/tires, tire levers, patch kits, and CO_2 cartridges. This equipment can be bound up and taped to this same area behind the seat post or carried in an empty water bottle with the top cut off that rides along in one of your water bottle cages.

BENTO BOX

Bento boxes that attach to the top tube are a great place to carry your nutrition, salt tabs, or anything else that you may need to access easily during the race.

CHOOSING THE RIGHT WHEELS AND TIRES

Not all wheels are appropriate for all terrain. When selecting wheels you will have to consider two main factors: the course and the conditions.

Traditional wheels

Traditional wheels will have a small rim and 32 spokes. These types of wheels are great for training as they are durable (you can hit pot holes with them), offer more wind resistance, and are cheaper. It's common for athletes to race with traditional wheels, but they will have two sets: one for training and the other for racing. Traditional wheels can be used in all conditions.

Deep section wheels

Deep section wheels have larger rim depth than a traditional wheel, which gives them aerodynamic quality. They also will have fewer numbers of spokes which provides less wind resistance through the center of the wheel. Deep section wheels generally come in rim depths of 4-10 cm, and are great for speed purposes (the larger the rim the more speed you will get), but are less stable than a traditional wheel in windy or hilly conditions.

Disc wheels

Disc wheels are designed to minimize aerodynamic drag, and are usually heavier than a traditional wheel. They are speedy because they have no spokes and therefore no wind resistance through the wheels. Disc wheels can be difficult to handle when climbing hills or in windy conditions. For this reason, organizations often ban or limit the use of discs only to the rear wheel of a bicycle. Disc wheels work well on a relatively flat terrain, with little or no wind.

Switching it up

It's very common for racers to have different wheels on the front and back of their bike. 11-time Ironman Champion Lisa Bentley says she always takes the time to determine which wheels are best for the course. "For Florida 70.3, which is flatter, I ride my Zipp disc back and Zipp 404 front, but for hilly St. Croix, I ride my Zipp 404's on front and back," she explains.

RUNNING EQUIPMENT

RUNNING SHOES

Light racing flats should be used in shorter distance races for your best performance. The longer the race gets, the more cushioning and support you should have in your shoes. A light weight trainer is a good shoe for longer distance races. As with the bike shoes, glue down the soles and lube where your feet will rub. Do your best to keep your shoes dry to avoid blisters.

ELASTIC LACES

Instead of losing valuable time in T2 to tie up your laces, elastic laces make it easy to slide your shoes on and off. Another benefit is that you never have to worry about your laces coming undone. Practice running with elastic laces before your race to adjust the fit – if they are too lose your feet will slip around, if they are too tight your feet will numb or swell.

RUNNING SOCKS

Some triathletes choose not to wear socks to save on transition time, but if you easily blister, or if your race is a longer distance, you should consider a good pair of socks, at least for the run leg. A few seconds of transition time is worth feet free of painful blisters.

RUNNING SHORTS

Running shorts are more of a preference than a necessity. Many triathletes will wear whatever they've swum in for the entire race, but if you prefer to be covered up, running shorts are lightweight and less bulky than biking shorts.

NUMBER BELT

A number belt is a thick elastic belt that you attach your race number to. Not only do you not have to worry about fussing around with pins but at T2, when your number must be switched from your back to your front, all it takes is a quick swivel.

CAP OR VISOR

A cap or visor in the run portion should be worn. They will protect against sun and will keep the sweat out of your eyes. If you are deciding between the two, remember that a cap is hotter than a visor, but it will protect better against sunburn and you can fill it with ice or sponges to help cool off.

© Kevin Light

RACE DAY CHECKLIST

RACE BAG	SWIM	BIKE	RUN
❑ PowerBars/gels	❑ Swim suit	❑ Helmet	❑ Shoes
❑ Cash, wallet, license	❑ Wetsuit	❑ Bike shorts	❑ Elastic laces
❑ iPod/music	❑ Body Glide	❑ Bike shoes	❑ Lace toggles
❑ Race instructions/maps	❑ Goggles	❑ Jersey	❑ Number belt
❑ Food/water	❑ Swim cap	❑ Cycle gloves	❑ Socks
❑ First aid, meds	❑ Sunscreen	❑ Anti-chafe	❑ Shorts
❑ Toilet bag	❑ Towel	❑ Sunglasses	❑ Singlet
❑ Heart rate monitor		❑ Pump	❑ Number, pins
❑ Towels		❑ Patch kit	❑ Cap
❑ Alarm clock		❑ Bottles	
❑ Floor pump		❑ Tools/lock	
❑ Bike cleaner, chain lube			
❑ Warm up clothes, jacket			
❑ Shoes, sandals			
❑ Tape, scissors, marker			

3 Be Ready for the Environment

© Dan Smith

You might not be able to predict the exact weather, but you can get a pretty good idea of what environmental conditions to expect on race day. Do your research; check the local weather in advance, see what the temperatures, humidity, precipitation, and prevailing winds are like; talk to people who have done the race before. Use this information to tweak your training accordingly. Environment is a huge factor in triathlons, especially the longer you go, so knowing what to expect and preparing for the specific race environment is the key to a successful race.

ACCLIMATIZING

WHAT IS ACCLIMATIZATION?

Air temperature, humidity, wind, and solar radiation are all things that can affect thermal balance. Acclimatization means getting your body used to these conditions, whether they are hot or cold, by simulating the environment through training. Because the majority of triathlons are held in warmer places, heat acclimatization should be considered part of you training plan, and if done properly, can mean improved tolerance and performance in the heat. In general, studies suggest that about 75 % of acclimatization occurs within 5 days of exposure to the environment. Full acclimatization occurs within 10-14 days.

HOW DOES ACCLIMATIZING HELP?

Acclimatizing helps evenly distribute blood between your skin and muscles so you have the oxygen needed for both oxygen contraction and blood flow to the skin for cooling. Your sweating threshold lowers, meaning you start sweating earlier and therefore start cooling earlier, and you also increase your sweat output. You will have a decrease in salt concentration in your sweat, as acclimatizing helps preserve electrolytes.

ACCLIMATIZE FROM HOME

Athletes preparing for a warm race may need to be creative in finding ways to replicate the race environment. Here are some proven ways to help with acclimatization.

Don't Push Yourself Too Hard

Training in the heat can be like training at altitude. It can reduce your training intensity and negatively affect your training. For example, if one runs at 2 pm when the sun is very intense, your heart rate may be 7-10 beats per minute higher than if you train at 6 am. Therefore you run slower and your muscles don't get the same quality of training in the afternoon. It is the same thing that has been shown with altitude training. Training high and living high doesn't work. You need to live high and train low. That way you adapt to altitude and train at sea level so you can hammer really hard.

Turn up the Heat!

If outdoor weather conditions aren't cooperating, then get inside and turn up that thermostat. If you're looking to compete in a hot and humid environment, it is necessary to acclimatize for both factors. Add some humidity by boiling a kettle in the room you are training in.

Wear Extra Layers

Wearing extra layers is a good way to increase your body's core temperature. When heading outside for a run, or if running indoors on a treadmill, try putting on a few extra layers of impermeable clothing.

Get to the Course Early

Some athletes will plan an early trip to the race site to get familiar with the weather and to train. But if planning an extra vacation doesn't fit your schedule you can also try to arrive early. Arriving at the race site a minimum of one week and ideally 10 days early is a huge help with acclimatization. Think of not only the physiological benefit, but the psychological benefit pre-training on the course will do for you!

Lose the A/C!

To maximize acclimatization, athletes should be exposed to the environmental conditions 24 hours a day. If the only exposure to hot conditions is during training and the athlete then returns to an air-conditioned environment, the effectiveness of acclimatization is reduced. It's recommended to spend a minimum of two weeks acclimatizing at the site of competition or in an environment very similar to that anticipated for competition.

© Dan Smith

WORKING OUT

Gordon Sleivert, Vice President of Sport Performance at the Canadian Sport Center Pacific, works with athletes in a heat chamber to help them acclimatize. The heat chamber was created to allow athletes to prepare for any event in an extreme environment, whether it is hot or cold, but was used greatly in helping Canadian triathletes prepare for the Olympics in Beijing.

"The most important thing in achieving heat adaptation is doing 5-7 days of consecutive training where you elevate and then hold your body temperature for 45-60 minutes," explains Sleivert. "As you adapt to this heat you will be able to do more. Use your heart rate as a guide."

Adding intensity to your workout can drive up your internal temperature quite a bit. Since monitoring your body temperature is hard to do from home, Sleivert suggests using intervals to get really hot, and then laying off to maintain core temperature after that.

Sleivert's Example Bike Workout
- Warm up with 10 minutes of easy spinning.

- Do five one minute intervals at 90 % max HR with one minute of rest in between.

- Continue with five minutes of easy spinning.

- Repeat.

- Back off and do easy spinning for 45-50 minutes at a comfortable pace at 60 % max HR.

SWEAT RATE

To get an accurate measurement of how much sweat will be lost on race day, it is important to simulate the environmental conditions and the amount of effort that will be put into the race. After ten days of acclimatization, your sweat rate almost doubles. You must match this by ensuring you are well hydrated.

In order to determine your sweat rate you must be weigh yourself pre and post effort (nude or minimal clothing is best), and any fluid consumed should be accounted for. Avoid going to the toilet until the measuring is completed. The simple formula to calculate sweat rate is as follows:

1. Weigh yourself prior to the exercise = "A" lbs.

2. Keep track of the amounts of fluids you consumed during exercise: "B" oz. consumed.

3. Weigh yourself upon completion of the exercise = "C" lbs.

4. Determine weight lost during exercise = "A" – "C" lbs. lost x 16 = "D" oz. lost.

5. Account for fluids consumed to determine your total sweat loss: "D" oz. sweat lost + "B" oz. fluids consumed = "E" oz. of total sweat loss.

6. Divide "E" (ounces of total sweat loss) by minutes of exercise for sweat rate per minute of exercise = ____ oz./minute sweat loss.

Example:
You weigh in at 150 pounds before the run, and weigh in at 145 after. During the run you consumed 8 oz. of water. You ran for 60 minutes.

(A – C) x 16 = D

(150 lbs – 145 lbs) x 16 = 80 oz.

D + B = E

80 oz. + 8 oz. = 88 oz. of total sweat loss

E/minutes of exercise = sweat rate

88 oz. /60 minutes = 1.47 oz. per minute

After determining your sweat rate it is easy to know how much fluid to consume during your exercise. In this case, 1.47 oz. is being lost per minute, so you should make up for this lost fluid by consuming a total of 88 oz. of fluid every hour of exercise. It is best to hydrate every 15 to 20 minutes.

© ASI Photos

HANDLING THE HEAT

The sport of triathlon is somewhat limited by the fact that it must be placed in locations where the water is warm enough to swim. More often than not this means that you will be racing in an area that is subject to hot and often humid weather conditions. A year of training can quickly be erased when an athlete is not prepared for a hot race.

Simple preparations like sunscreen, a visor, cool clothing, and hydrating properly can be a great help. Keep yourself cool by pouring water on your head, neck, back, and arms (try not to soak your shoes) and utilize ice or sponges in the back and front of your racing suit. Heat is uncomfortable, but it will be tough on everyone – you are not alone.

BE FIT

The best performances in the heat tend to come from the athletes with the most fitness. The effects of the heat will become exponential if the athlete's physiology is already struggling with the workload. Even under the best conditions heat production in the muscles increases with the intensity of the activity. Achieving optimal fitness will not only maximize performance, but will also maintain plasma volume in the blood which results in a lower heart rate and will maintain oxygen delivery to working muscles. All of these factors lead to a lower core temperature minimizing heat stress and discomfort.

WEAR COOL CLOTHING

What you choose to wear can have a big impact on your cooling efficiency. Light colors reflect the light causing the athlete to be cooler than if they chose dark clothing. The fit and weight of clothing also affects an athlete's temperature. A looser fit and lighter fabric (such as DriFit or CoolMax) increases air circulation and helps to keep sweat away from the body. If possible, wear your biking clothes under your wetsuit. This will not only aid in cooling, but will help you whiz through T1. Wearing a visor on the run is also more efficient than a hat because much of your body heat will be lost through your head.

HAVE COOLING STRATEGIES

Keep yourself cool by drinking cold fluids. Remember that it is better for cooling to put a fluid "in you" rather than "on you" although ideally you can do both. External cooling can be achieved by using water, ice, or sponges in critical areas such as the back of the head, neck, and chest. It's important to use sunscreen as sunburned skin promotes dehydration and doesn't regulate temperature as well as normal skin.

REHYDRATE AND RECOVER

Great recovery is critical for your regeneration and will lead to you becoming faster and stronger as the body adapts and super-compensates. Within the first 20 minutes after exercise, rehydrate with at least 2-3 cups of electrolyte drink for every pound of body weight lost. You could get three times the regeneration if you do this immediately as opposed to waiting. Lower your body temperature back down as soon as possible by moving to a cooler area out of the sun with access to water and ice. It is also important to replace your glucose stores with easily digestible foods such as fruit. Try to get a full meal including complex carbohydrates and proteins within 2-3 hours of the activity.

COPING WITH THE COLD

It is less common for triathlons to be held in cold climates, but you can never rely on the weather to be warm all of the time. Make sure you are prepared for both conditions just in case the weather forecaster does not have something pleasant to say on race day. Here are a few ideas to prepare:

BRING WARM CLOTHES TO THE START

Regardless of the air temperature, wear or bring along a kit of warm clothes with a small bag. Your kit should include a long sleeve shirt, warm jacket, hat, gloves, and sock. You may want to wear old clothes in case you never see them again, but there is a very good chance you can pass it off to a friend or family member. If not, mark your bag with your name and it may be there once your race is over.

© Dan Smith

WETSUIT WARM-UP FOR A NON-WETSUIT SWIM?

Race morning conditions can be deceiving, particularly when the water is barely warm enough to be deemed a non-wetsuit legal swim however cool the air is. This is often when we see athletes freeze up the most because the direct body exposure to the water lowers their body temperature and then exposure to the cool air after the warm-up, and again on the bike, really gives them a chill. A great way to prevent this is to bring your wetsuit to the race and use it for the warm-up. The wetsuit will keep you warm and allow you to get a good warm-up in. Once you have finished your warm up and you can either leave the suit on to stay warm or put on some warm clothing until the race is ready to begin.

WARM UP RIGHT

A good warm up will allow you to be prepared for cooler conditions because working muscles produce heat. This along with good circulation will increase your body's temperature. You should always get in the water for a warm-up no matter how cold you think it is. This warm-up will aid with the overall activation of the muscles to produce heat and it will also prevent the shock factor of entering very cold water at the beginning of the race which will often leave athletes gasping for air and more focused on survival rather than performance. Your warm-up on race day should start with the legs an hour before the race, either a 10-15 run or ride, and then a swim warm-up 20-30 minutes before race start. If you are not allowed in the water, you can substitute the swim with a series of arm swings and circles. A set of swim stretch cords or surgical tubing will help provide some resistance if you are serious about your warm-up.

OTHER STRATEGIES TO STAY WARM ON THE SWIM

A few other tricks to stay warm on the swim are:

*   Wear 2 swims caps.

*   Apply Vaseline wherever there is exposed skin – it will act as a layer of protection (avoid the palms of the hands so you can feel the water).

*   Wear a neoprene cap (in extremely cold water conditions).

The open water swim can be the most intimidating thing about competing in cold weather. Don't let the water temperature stress you out. Prepare yourself in warm-up by putting your head under the water. This way the water temperature won't come as a shock and affect your start, and you'll likely find that it's not as cold as you thought.

DRESS IN LIGHT LAYERS

Chances are that you are going to heat up at some point in the race. When preparing for the bike, dress in light layers or pieces that can be easily removed rather than one heavy layer. Stay away from cotton—when cotton gets wet it is heavy, doesn't insulate and dries slowly. Also avoid items that you have to pull on over your head – this is very difficult with wet and tired arms. Arm and legs warmers are ideal if you are worried about the cold. They can be

© Mike Byrne

put on and taken off very easily allowing you to shed them later on if you are heating up but make sure you've practiced putting on and taking off these items before the race. If you are very prone to the cold, slip on a light, tight-fitting technical jacket or vest before you go on to the bike to break the wind. Extreme conditions may warrant gloves, head band, and bootie/toe covers for your cycling shoes. As mentioned in the swim, Vaseline can also provide a nice layer if you decide to ride in the same racing suit that you swam in.

© SI Photography

HALEY COOPER— "I LOVE CRAPPY CONDITIONS"

While many athletes dread doing a triathlon in bad weather, pro triathlete Haley Cooper actually prefers it. And although this may seem odd in the eyes of many, the reasoning behind her love for lousy weather is quite simple.

"My favorite races are in crappy conditions because I live and grew up in a colder climate area where we can have pretty hard winters," she explains.

Cooper is from Spokane, Washington, where it is not rare for temperatures to drop into the negatives during the winter months. Cooper admits that she struggles in heat, so whenever a colder climate triathlon rolls around, she takes advantage of the opportunity to show up her competition.

"I love headwinds in races. All I have to do is put my head down and pedal while everyone else is demoralized by the wind," says Cooper. "The crummier the better because it's intimidating for people."

So the next time you're faced with less than ideal environmental conditions in a race, it wouldn't be a bad idea to make like Haley and just put it out of your mind and race, you might be surprised at what an advantage this has over everyone else.

OTHER FACTORS

WAVES!

In rough water conditions, many athletes will attempt to fight the waves by lifting their head and shoulders out of the water. The best strategy is to keep your head low in the water and focus on keeping your arm in touch with the water and increase your stroke rate slightly even though you may feel like you are 'spinning your wheels.' Drafting behind another swimmer is also another good strategy and remember to always remain calm – you're swimming much better than you think you are and the waves are not dangerous. Sometimes you will need to fight the waves and current for a portion of the swim, but you will likely get rewarded with a nice ride back. Don't become discouraged!

© Mark Oleksyn

© Sheila Campbell

BIKING WITH WIND

Just like with heat, the best way to train for a windy race is to practice in similar conditions. Unfortunately replicating windy weather, like that in Kona or any other windy place, is much harder than turning up the heater. Try incorporating lower cadence strength workouts into your bike training and do longer intervals of pedaling one constant gear. You should also get used to being in the aero position for long periods of time – this will minimize your body's drag in the wind. And just like the waves on the swim, work hard when there is a head wind because often you will get the tail wind once you make a turn and it is much harder to make up time on your competitors in a tail wind. If you experience crosswinds, remain low on your bike – it is much more stable this way even though the instinct will be to sit up higher. Keep a good cadence because this will also keep the bike stable and look down the road to see other riders that may be getting gusts of wind so you know what is coming.

Aero wheels are more susceptible to picking up crosswinds and moving you around, especially if you are a smaller rider who will get blown around easily. If you know you will be facing some strong winds, travel to your event with two sets of wheels in case a last minute adjustment needs to take place. Disc wheels will pick up the most wind and are not allowed on some courses but a 4-6cm deep rim on the front wheel and a 6-8cm rim on the back should be safe on almost any course. It also is useful to have an alternative drinking system that will allow you to keep both hands on the wheel, and avoid any clothing that is going to flap in the wind. On courses with a lot of crosswinds, an aero helmet can catch a lot of wind, so it's best to stick with a regular model.

ALLERGIES

Obviously the easiest way to prevent allergy symptoms is to avoid the allergens altogether, but since triathlons take place outdoors, this can be difficult. Do some investigating and know in advance if there is anything that would trigger an allergic reaction and bring meds accordingly.

© fotolia

4 Race Week and Race Day Nutrition

Food is more than just food for triathletes. It's fuel. Picture a high performing race car that runs out of gas and oil. No matter how fast and capable of performance that car is, when it is running out of gas it will sputter on fumes, stop performing and eventually come to a stop. When it runs out of oil it will seize. This couldn't be more true for the human athlete who will experience decreased performance without the proper calories and hydration, and will sometimes be relegated to a walk or stopping when completely depleted. Every triathlete is very different in this regard, so it's important to find what works best for you – what fuels you best, how much, what goes down the smoothest, what digests the best – and make it a routine.

THE 3 ESSENTIALS

Race nutrition is comprised of water (hydration), electrolytes (salts), andfood (carbohydrates, protein, fat), each of which plays a vital role in a triathlete's body.

HYDRATION

Water makes up about 70 percent of our total body weight. Since blood is 90 percent water and muscle is made up of 75 percent water, it is obvious that water is the most essential nutrient for our bodies. Because this water is continually being depleted from the body through functions such as sweating, going to the toilet, and breathing – and at a much faster rate during exercise – it needs to be replenished. The average non-exercising person will need to consume about 2 liters of water a day to make up for lost fluids. Exercising triathletes can expend this every hour. Hydration enables many of the physiological systems in the body that promote performance to function.

© fotolia, salam

The body keeps cool during exercise by sweating. Because triathletes are exercising for such long periods of time, it's not uncommon to lose 2-3 % of bodyweight through sweating. Loss of this much water can significantly reduce endurance performance.

It is common for triathletes during training or racing to only replace about 50 % of lost fluids. The average fluid loss through sweating can be as high as 40-64 oz. (1.5-2 liters) per hour of exercise. That being said, the maximum absorption rate is only 26 – 34 oz (800 ml – 1 liter) per hour during exercise, thus, despite our best efforts, slight dehydration will occur. It is important to pay close attention to the signs of mild dehydration to improve performance and prevent damage to your body.

SIGNS OF DEHYDRATION

- Headaches

- Fatigue

- Irritability

- Loss of appetite

- Flushed skin

- Dizziness

- Increased body temperature

- Small amount of dark urine

As an athlete, you should make it a goal to stay within +/-2 % of your body weight. To ensure you are well hydrated for an event, follow these tips:

1. Be sure to drink 16-25 oz (500-750 ml) of a carbohydrate drink and/or water 2-3 hours before the event.

2. In the hour leading up to the event it is best to avoid carbohydrate drinks as they can be a bit harder on the stomach. One hour before exercise, drink 10-18 oz (250-500 ml) of water.

3. Do not drink again until after you visit the toilet 10-15 min before start time. Consume another 8-10 oz (250 ml) of water and this will be absorbed as you start your effort before it ever reaches the bladder.

4. During the race aim to consume 8-10 oz (200-250 ml) of a 6-8 % solution of a carbohydrate drink with electrolyte every 15-20 minutes during exercise. Data suggests that nearly half of a triathlete's fluid loss occurs during the run because of increased muscle activity and decreased convective air cooling as compared to the bike, so keep well hydrated on the bike and don't ignore the water stations on the run.

PRACTICE HYDRATING IN TRAINING

In order to achieve the best hydration possible during a race it is best to practice in training by aiming to replace fluids by 80 %. This is equal to about a 1 % loss of body weight. This is important to practice because it may take some time for

© SI Photography

your stomach to get used to handling that kind of volume during exercise. To figure out how much water you should be consuming during exercise, it's necessary to determine your sweat rate (see chapter 3).

ELECTROLYTES

Many heart and nerve functions, muscle control and coordination, and the body's ability to absorb fluids all depend on a healthy balance of electrolytes – electrically charged ions commonly known as salts.

The most common electrolytes in the body are sodium, potassium, magnesium, chloride and calcium. If the duration of exercise exceeds an hour, electrolyte solutions are needed and are commonly taken in the form of sports drinks or salt tabs. Sports drinks contain added potassium and sodium to help restore the body's proper electrolyte balance after intense physical exertion.

Electrolyte loss is different for different people, but is generally between 500-1200 mg per hour of exercise. A good way to get an idea of how much electrolytes you are losing during exercise is to look for a white, salty substance on your clothes. If you notice salt on your clothing after workouts you are probably a "salty sweater" and should pay careful attention to electrolyte intake.

Heavy sweaters, those who have sweat rates in excess of 1.5-2 pounds, should also be aware that additional electrolytes will be needed.

If you are heading into a hot race you can eat saltier foods during the week and add some additional table salt to your meals. Salt pills can also be used during the race for athletes that require additional electrolytes. Remember to practice these strategies in training!

FOOD

Energy from food comes in three forms: carbohydrates, protein and fats. Some of this energy is stored in the body so that muscles and organs can use them as an immediate source of energy. Foods you eat just before or during exercise can also fuel muscles.

CARBOHYDRATES

Carbohydrates are the most important form of energy for working muscles. Out of the three forms of energy, carbohydrates burn the fastest (up to three times faster than the energy from fat) and are the easiest to digest and absorb during physical activity.

The main function of carbohydrates is to provide energy, although they have many other functions. The downside is that the body can store a limited supply of carbs at a given time. Carbohydrates have 4 calories per gram.

UP YOUR CARBS

If your duration of effort is over 60-90 minutes, ingesting carbohydrate is required and beneficial for performance. Hot weather conditions will increase the need for carbohydrates as the fuel requirements for the body will increase with hot conditions. Carbohydrates can be gained through sports drinks as mentioned above although larger sources will be required in the heat. Additional carbs can come through higher carb solutions, bars, and gels. The range will vary with size of the athlete but generally speaking you should aim for a minimum of 200-300 calories and 70 grams of carbs (200 in cooler conditions or shorter races, 300 in hotter conditions or longer distance races). The following table demonstrates some suggestions on calorie and carb intakes for a hot or longer race:

Activity Length	Calories	Carbs	Suggested Source
1 hour	0	0	Water only (min 1 bottle/hour)
2 hours	250	50 g	1 Sports Drink (500ml), 1 Gel
3 hours	500	140 g	2 Sports Drinks, 2 Gels
4 hours	850	210 g	3 Sports Drinks, 1 Bar, 2 Gels
5 hours	1200	280 g	4 Sports Drinks, 2 Bars, 2 Gels
6 hours	1500	350 g	4 Sports Drinks, 3 Bars, 3 Gels

Substitutions:
1 Sports Drink = 1.5 Gel
2 Sports Drinks = 1 Bar + 1 Gel
1 Bar = 2 Gels

* The above recommendations do not address fluid intake. In general consuming about 800ml-1l/hour of fluid is recommended.

PROTEIN

Protein's role is to build and repair body tissues. It also helps to produce enzymes and hormones. Protein should comprise about 15 % of your daily caloric intake, and has 4 calories per gram. Protein is a less efficient form of energy compared to carbohydrates, and is generally found in animal meat, dairy products, nuts, and some vegetables.

FAT

Fat provides a stored form of energy, contributes to healthy skin, and is part of the structure of hormones and cell membranes. It is necessary for organ function, and allows vitamins A, D, E and K to be absorbed into the body. Fat has a slow energy release; therefore, high fat diets can lead to weight gain, obesity, and the development of heart disease and certain cancers. In a triathlete's diet, about 20 % of caloric intake should come from fat. Fat has 9 calories per gram.

RACE WEEK

CARBO LOADING

The average male can store 1500-1900 kcals of carbohydrates: 60-80 kcal in blood, 360-440 in liver, and 1300-1400 in muscles. Hours of exercise can deplete the liver and muscle glycogen (stored carbohydrate) levels substantially. Obvious signs of depletion are heavy, tired muscles, poor performance, and fatigue.

Sports nutritionists recommend increasing carbohydrate intake to at least 9-10 grams per kilogram of bodyweight 2-3 days before an event. This should be achieved by altering your training load and diet over a seven day period before the race. Moderate training and normal diet should be followed for the first four days. For the remaining three days, low to moderate intensity exercise and a high carbohydrate diet should be followed.

Carbo-loading also includes reducing your training load and resting the muscles to allow them to become completely loaded with glycogen. Since you want to start the race with as much glycogen as possible, resting and low to moderate intensity exercise is as important as eating in the process of super-compensation.

Knowing how many carbohydrates to consume before, during, and after competition and training is important in athletic performance. If completed properly, carbo-loading can almost double the normal amount of stored carbohydrate found in a trained person.

Race Week Rules

- Keep a consistent routine.
- Increase hydration slightly and be sure to include electrolytes.
- Avoid new foods.
- Don't overeat.

RACE MORNING

1. Breakfast should be what you would normally eat before heading out for a long day of training, and should be between 500-1000 calories, possibly more if you are accustomed to it. Some athletes prefer to get their race morning calories from liquids rather than solids. If this is the case, many meal replacement drinks are available. Your breakfast should consist of some protein, but limit fiber as it provides little energy and bulks up waste products.

2. Hydrate with a sports drink until urine is light yellow up to one hour before the race.

3. If you feel the need to put a little something in your stomach, a snack can be consumed about 1 hour before race start. After this time don't eat or drink anything in the hour leading up to the race until 10 minutes before start where you should include some light hydration (one cup of water – 250 ml – half of a small water bottle).

YOUR RACE PLAN

Know what and when you will eat and drink leading up to and during the race and have it laid out in a plan. Typically a well hydrated athlete will have between 1.5-2 small water bottles/hour along with 250-300 calories/hour. The amount of

Race Day Hydration/Nutrition Plan

Name: _____

Updated: _____

Scenario: (Cold/Warm/Hot), Air Temp _____ C/F, Humidity: (low/Med/High)

Known Sweat Rates:
Swim: _____ (oz/hr)   Bike _____ (oz/Hr)   Run _____ (oz/hr)

Event	Time	Food	Fluids	Volume (l)	Calories	Carbs (g)	Sodium (mg)
Pre-Race	3-2 hrs						
	2 hr-15 min						
	15-0 min						
Race	0 min						
Swim							
Bike (hourly)							
Run (hourly)							
Post-Race	0-3 hrs						

electrolytes (salt) you take in will also be a factor – go with 600-1000 mg of sodium/hour for hot conditions to ensure proper absorption of fluids. Take in your liquids every 15-20 min and your calories every 20-30 minutes on a consistent basis. Your body is an engine that requires fuel – don't run out of gas!

BONKING

In endurance sports, bonking or "hitting the wall" describes a condition caused by the depletion of glycogen (stored energy) in the liver and muscles. Bonking is sudden fatigue and loss of energy.

Mild instances can be remedied by brief rest and ingestions of food and drinks that contain carbohydrates. Bonking can be avoided altogether by ensuring that glycogen levels are high when exercise begins, and are maintained throughout exercise.

The three main ways to avoid "hitting the wall" are:

- Carbo loading
- Ingesting carbs throughout exercise
- Lowering the intensity of exercise

RACING – RULES OF THUMB

1. Have a Race Nutrition Plan.

2. Follow Pre-Race plan for Nutrition/Hydration.

3. Take only water in T-1.

4. Wait until 10 min into bike before eating.

5. Consume about 2/3 of your food on the bike.

6. It is better to absorb calories from solid sources and switch to gels/liquids as the race goes on.

7. Use only tried and true carb foods in the race.

8. Drink every 15 to 20 min and eat every 20 to 30 min, depending on race.

9. Keep a regular flow of nutrition into your stomach on the bike and run.

10. Do not overeat or -drink during the race to prevent sloshing.

11. Reduce intensity if body cannot accept foods.

12. Have a contingency plan if foods don't work.

IRONMAN NUTRITION

In an Ironman event it's impossible to consume enough to make up for the calories used. For example, a 150-pound person will use 8775 calories in 10 hours of exercise, but will only be able to consume 3280 calories in return. Generally an athlete competing in an Ironman should take in between 3000-6000 calories depending on weight. About 2/3 of your total calories should be consumed on the bike, while the other 1/3 should be consumed during the run. It is interesting to note that studies have shown that caloric intake should be based on the distance of the event and the athlete's weight, not the total number of hours it will take to complete the distance. This is based on assumption that calories will be utilized at a higher rate if the athlete is going faster so more will be needed per hour, therefore the same overall amount as an athlete racing slower using less calories. This will still be a very individual measurement that needs to be practiced in training and athletes that are competing over longer distances should plan to have some additional calories available if needed. The following chart outlines Ironman nutrition needs with the weight of an athlete and hours of exercise considered to determine an hourly rate.

Weight (lb)	Hours of exercise	Total cals burned	Cal intake needed per hour	Total cals needed
120	10	7020	305	3050
	12	7020	262	3144
	15	7020	218	3270
150	10	8775	382	3820
	12	8775	327	3924
	14	8775	273	3822
180	10	10530	458	4580
	12	10530	393	4716
	15	10530	327	4905

CARRYING YOUR NUTRITION

Bike nutrition can be stored in your jersey pockets or a saddle bag, but a bento box mounted to your top tube is highly recommended. Bottle cages on both your seat tube and down tube should be utilized along with an additional hydration system whether it be attach to your aero bars, frame mounted, or rear mounted. There is also the option of wearing a hydration pack on your back if

© SI Photography

you are seriously concerned about your hydration. Salt tabs can be stored in an easy-to-open plastic container (try one that normally holds gum or candy!) and then placed in your bento box or jersey pocket. Remember that all nutrition and hydration should be firmly secured on your bike because bumpy roads have a tendency to launch these critical items off of your bike. For the run fuel belts can be used, and for women, gels and bars can be stuffed into your sports bra.

POST RACE

1. Eat a high glycemic carbohydrate and protein combination within 30 min post-workout (check the race finish area for foods like sandwiches and pizza). This will aid in restoring your blood sugar levels and repairing muscles.

2. Replace lost fluids and electrolytes immediately post-workout. Most athletes will finish in a state of dehydration, so consuming a 20-24 oz (600-700 ml) combo of fluid and electrolytes will help to rehydrate.

3. Continue to replenish your glycogen stores by eating small meals rich in carbohydrates every 2-3 hours post-exercise.

NUTRITION MISTAKES TO AVOID

- Using new or untested products on race day.

- Not having a nutrition plan for race day.

- Not having an adequate breakfast. A healthy breakfast will refuel your body, set your blood sugar level for the day, start the absorption process, and give you the energy you need to operate and concentrate.

- Not evenly pacing the nutrition and hydration consumption in the race; starting on the bike each 15-20 min for hydration, 20-30 min for calories. A little trick – set your countdown timer as a reminder.

- Not enough electrolytes during the race.

- Not being self dependent and relying on the race-supplied nutrition and hydration – that may or may not be there when you need it.

- Using improper carrying devices for the nutrition and hydration.

- Athletes tend to pay a ton of attention to carbs and forget about protein. Triathletes should eat at least 1/2 to 3/4 of a gram of protein per pound of body weight. This means a 150 lb person should be eating 75-112 grams of protein a day.

- Not making the adjustment for hotter days – more is needed.

- Don't forget about your post-workout nutrition. It's important to get a meal in within 30 minutes after you exercise to help your body recover.

- Avoid caffeine and alcohol post race as they are diuretics and will cause dehydration.

© Mark Creery

© SI Photography

5   Race Morning

The day has finally arrived. In just a few short hours you will be standing at the start line and chances are that nerves are setting in. Race morning can be stressful if you're not fully ready, but if you are prepared you can turn that nervous energy into excitement. Being organized the day before your race, getting a good sleep, eating a good breakfast, and doing a proper warm-up— all of these things will not only better your morning, but they will ultimately better your race too.

WAKING

The start of your race morning shouldn't be any different than your typical morning although it may happen a bit earlier. Do as you usually would to get yourself activated – if you have a shower, then shower. If you check your e-mail, then check your e-mail – the only difference is that because you are on a strict schedule, soon after waking you should be eating. You should wake up at least 2.5-3 hours before the event, and eat breakfast no later than 2 hours before race start.

IMPROVE SLEEP QUALITY

Not everyone is a morning person. To ensure you wake up on the right side of the bed on race day, follow these guidelines to improve your sleep.

Play background music or noise – monotonous sounds like waves help drown out distractions.

Sleep in complete darkness – the dark is a stimulus for melatonin (the hormone that creates sleepiness).

Avoid high levels of mental stimulation before bed time – instead of TV, problem solving or over-thinking, try reading, listening to music or having a warm bath instead.

Keep your sleeping temperature around 21 degrees Celsius (70 Fahrenheit) – being overly hot or cold will interfere with your ability to fall asleep.

Don't drink fluids within 2 hours before bed time – this way you won't have to wake up in the middle of the night to go to the bathroom and potentially not be able to fall back asleep.

Establish a pre-bed routine and keep to it – go to sleep and wake up at the same times during the week so your schedule is intact.

Make sure everything you've assembled the night before comes with you! As you are headed out the door perform a quick check.

HEATHER GOLLNICK'S MORNING ROUTINE

On race morning athletes must find ways to wake themselves up and get pumped about the race ahead of them. Five-time Ironman Champion, Heather Gollnick has a special way to do this.

"I always get up really early and go for a little jog," says Gollnick. "This gets my body going then I come back, use the restroom, have breakfast, and get ready for the race. It's only about 5-10 minutes, but it's at four in the morning! It wakes me up and gets me going."

NUTRITION AND HYDRATION BEFORE THE RACE

Practice the following routine on race morning:

1. **As soon as you wake up** begin hydrating with electrolytes and continue to do so regularly.

2. Eat a normal breakfast of something you're accustomed to **2-3 hours before the race**, and if possible, throw a little protein in there. The protein helps to evenly pace the absorption, and thereby vitalizing carbohydrates over a longer period of time.

3. **One hour before the race** have a snack (energy bar or sports drink), and hydrate again.

4. Don't hydrate after this until about 10-15 minutes before race start. Everything you drank up to one hour before the race will be either utilized or in the bladder by **10-15 minutes before race start**. Go to the toilet. After this, consume 250 ml of fluid (half a water bottle) and you should also have your last intake of calories – this can be in the form of a gel or a sports drink (although the sports drink can sometimes be harder on your stomach). The fluid will never reach the bladder, as it will be utilized right away once you start racing.

Following this race formula will allow you to be fueled and hydrated, and you won't have to go to the bathroom during the race!

FINAL CHECKS

Arrive at the site early enough to get a decent parking space, give yourself time to walk to the start area, set up, and do a good warm-up. Ideally be in transition at your bike 90 minutes before race start. Go to the bathroom. Get your body numbered and get your timing chip. In transition do an equipment check:

- Are the seat, headset, and aerobars tight?

- Is the bike in an easy gear for takeoff?

- Are the brake pads free from rubbing against the rims and the wheels not rubbing against the frame?

- Are the tires inflated to the proper PSI?

- Are the spare kit, bottles, nutrition, and anything else attached to bike secure?

- Is the helmet ready to go, accessible, and on the bike?

- Are the helmet chin straps the proper length, is the clasp working?

- If shoes are left clipped to pedals are they easily accessible?

- Is everything lubed/powdered and ready to go?

- Are clothes and shoes ready to go in transition? Race number? Hat? Run nutrition/hydration?

WARM-UPS

Warming up on race day is a must so avoid the temptation not to do it! Chances are that you warm up for every other workout where you will be raising your effort in practice, so race day is no exception. A vigorous warm up should be planned – be confident even if your head is saying to conserve your energy! It will help you perform better.

WARM-UP BENEFITS

Increased Muscle Temperature

During a warm-up, the temperature of the muscles being used is increased. Warmer muscles mean better contraction, and better contraction means that your speed and strength will be enhanced. Also, when your muscles are warm, the probability of overstretching and causing injury is far less.

Increased Body Temperature

By increasing your body temperature you are increasing muscle elasticity and reducing the risk of strains and pulls.

Dilated Blood Vessels

Dilated blood vessels reduce resistance in blood flow and lowers stress on the heart.

Better Cooling

When you warm up, your body begins its cooling process (sweating). This will help to prevent overheating early in the race.

Increased Blood Temperature

The temperature of blood increases as it travels through the muscles, and as blood temperature rises, the amount of oxygen it can hold becomes reduced.

The oxygen that normally would be carried through the blood is now made available to the working muscles, enhancing endurance and performance.

Improved Range of Motion

When you warm up, the range of motion around your joints is increased, meaning you won't be stiff and uncomfortable when you start racing.

Hormonal Changes

When warming up, your body increases its production of hormones responsible for regulating energy production, making more carbohydrates and fatty acids available for energy production.

Mental Preparation

The warm up is a good time to mentally prepare for an event by clearing the mind, increasing focus, and reviewing skills and strategies.

SUGGESTED WARM-UPS

With all the chaos of race morning you will need to plan well so that you don't sacrifice your warm-up time. Generally we would suggest warming up your legs 60 minutes before your race start and then warming up for the swim 30 minutes before your race start. Allow 10-15 minutes for warm-up which, when completed, will still give ample time to get exit the water, relax, have a quick drink, and make swim gear adjustments. Remember to have some warm clothes when you come out of the water.

Some triathlons do not allow for an open water swim warm-up, so we have included two suggested warm-up scenarios based on whether you are allowed in the water or not.

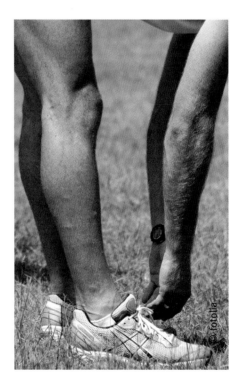

SCENARIO #1 – SWIM WARM-UP IS ALLOWED

Legs/Activation (60 minutes prior to race)

- Light 10-15min run or bike (personal preference) and include 4 x 30s pick ups to your race pace, each one gets slightly faster
- Light stretching

Swim (30 minutes prior to race)

- 2-3 minutes of arm circles and light stretching on shore
- 5 minutes of relaxed swimming and mixed stroke to loosen up
- 6 x 30 strokes of drills that make you feel the water followed by 20 strokes of freestyle
- 8 x 20 vigorous strokes for activation with 20 strokes of smooth easy freestyle between
- 2 minutes of easy swimming to flush

SCENARIO #2 – SWIM WARM-UP IS NOT ALLOWED

Legs/Activation (60 minutes prior to race)

- Same as above

Dryland Swim (20 minutes prior to start)

- 10 minutes of arm swings and circles routine (increase effort as you go so that HR rises):
  - Both arms forward circles
  - Single arm each forward circles
  - Both arms backwards circles
  - Single arm each backward circles
  - Bent over double arm pull back
  - Bent over freestyle simulation
  - Standing trunk rotation with bent arms
- Stretch cords can also be used (see opposite)
- Light stretching

© fotolia

STRETCH CORDS

A good way to simulate a swim warm-up is with stretch cords. An elastic cord or surgical tubing can be tied to an object to create resistance. The cords can be tied in a loop to hold your hands or attached to paddles so that you can mimic your swim stroke. Here are some suggested movements:

Double arm: Bend over at the waist and lower your head. With arms straight and outstretched in front of you, pull your arms down to your sides simultaneously. Finish with your hands past your hips.

Single arm: Same as above, but alternate one arm at a time in a freestyle swim pattern.

Tricep pull-back: Similar to Double arm but start with your hands at your sides and your elbows tucked in.

Chest fly: Stand upright with arms outstretched in front of you. Keep your arms at chest height, pull each arm to the side and back until your hands are in line with your shoulders.

Reverse fly: Stand upright and face away from where the cords are tied. Outstretch your arms at shoulder level. Keep your arms at shoulder height, press your hands together in front of your chest.

DAY OF RACE STRATEGY PLAN

Sometimes it is helpful to plan out your race morning to prepare mentally and physically for your race. Here is a sample morning plan.

Goals				Actions	
Time before event	Desired Feelings	Location	Who you want to be with	Action	Alternatives
3.5 hrs	relaxed	in bed	alone	waking up, start hydrating	
3 hrs	relaxed	hotel room (have my own food)	other athletes/ family	eating breakfast (juice, water, bagel w/jam, coffee, banana, starting to prepare bag	eating in restaurant
2.5 hrs	awake, exited but still calm	hotel room	alone	shower, dressing, re-check race bag, pump tires, washroom	
2 hrs	focused and feeling prepared	travel to race site	w/athletes but tuned out by music	mental rehearsal, listening to music, hydrating, toilet	
1.5 hrs	focused and feeling prepared	at race site	Coach/ family	reviewing race plan and goals-any changes with weather, strategy etc.	

1-1.5 hrs	positive and energized	in transitions	alone	setting up transition, walk transition area, body numbering, washroom, drinking water, have one gel	
1 hr	positive and energized	bike course	alone, maybe with one other athlete	Legs warm-up: short building bike with few short pick ups, toilet, then hydrate	run
30 min	positive and energized	in water	alone	in water warming up, get out and practice a few starts	
15 min	positive and energized	beside start	Coach or family	last minute encouragement, go to toilet, warm clothes	self motivation
10 min	positive and energized	in water	alone or team mates	drink 250 ml fluid, gel, stay loose	at start mentally rehearsing
5 min	positive and energized	at start	alone	self talk	

© Dan Smith

6 Swim Preparation

The swim, although the shortest part of a triathlon, can be very important in setting yourself up for a strong bike and run performance in the race. A good swim can set the tone and rhythm for the rest of your race and provide a positive confidence that can carry on throughout the day. Even if the swim is not your natural strength, it still warrants strong training, preparation, and race day tactics.

RACE WEEK PREPARATION

ENVIRONMENTAL CONDITIONS

It's important to check into the weather conditions before you hit the water on race day. Know what to expect when it comes to temperature of the water and the air, as well as normal wind patterns, currents and tides. Also visit the site a few days before the race and check out the sun at race time – if it is close to the horizon in any of the directions you are swimming, plan to have tinted goggles for better vision.

PREPARE MENTALLY

The day before your event is an ideal time to mentally think through the race. Revisit memories of successful workouts or races where you really felt like you were swimming high on the water with great rhythm and lock these images in. How do you want to feel when you are in the water? What are your keys for success?

KNOW THE SWIM COURSE AND SEGMENT

Know the features of your race course such as the location and distance between the buoys, turns, how the water moves (currents or waves), sun position, and local landmarks. Using this, strategically segment the course into small pieces and have a particular goal for each section that you can implement on race day. This will also help you avoid losing focus and "daydreaming" during the middle sections of the course.

KEY RACE WEEK WORKOUTS

The following workout is designed to be shorter in duration but still include some efforts that simulate those of the race and will keep your body activated. Plan this swim workout for mid-week in and in the open water if possible. The purpose of this workout is to:

- provide an opportunity to practice your race day warm up.

- rehearse different effort sections of your race.

- provide fitness maintenance (maybe even a little fitness gain) with ample ability to recover and be ready for race day.

Warm-up:
- Practice your race day warm-up

- Start with arm swings on shore then 600 (10min) as:

- 2-3 minutes of arm circles and light stretching on shore

- 5 minutes of relaxed swimming and mixed stroke to loosen up

- 6 x 30 strokes of drills that make you feel the water followed by 20 strokes of freestyle

- 8 x 20 vigorous strokes for activation with 20 strokes of smooth easy freestyle between

- 2 minutes of easy swimming to flush

Main Set:
- 1 x 300 (5 min) of steady swimming with 60 seconds of recovery

- 1 x 500 (7 min) at moderate race pace with 2 minutes of recovery

- 1 x 300 (5 min) at your starting speed (strongest one) with 60 seconds of recovery

Cool-down:
- 5-10 minutes of easy swimming including rotational drills

- Practice exit and wetsuit removal (if race is a wetsuit-legal swim)

The following set is designed for the pool and can be a great way to keep in touch with your speed and pacing in a controlled environment:

Warm-up:

300 free

200 reverse IM (2 x 25 of free, breast, back, fly)

100 kick

200 free breathe every 5 strokes

200 IM (2 x 25 of fly, back, breast, free)

8 x 50 as 20 fast/30 easy, steady, long

Main Set:

4 x 100 with 20s Recovery

100 choice with 60s Recovery

4 x 100 faster than set 1

100 choice with 60s Recovery

4 x 100 faster than set 2

100 choice with 60s Recovery

Cool-down:

200 choice drill, 300 choice stroke

© Mike Byrne

START STRATEGIES AND PACING

WARM-UP

A warm-up is a critical part of any good athletic performance. You probably warm-up in swim practice, so don't exclude it on race day. Attempt to organize yourself so that you arrive at the swim start ready to go 30 minutes prior to race start. Allow 10-15 minutes for warm-up which, when completed, will still give ample time to get exit the water, relax, have a quick drink, and make swim gear adjustments. If it is a wetsuit-legal swim, this is a good time to ensure your wetsuit is pulled up in the crotch and arms so there is free movement across the shoulders.

STARTING POSITION

Although placing yourself in a more aggressive starting position might make you uncomfortable, it's much better to have swimmers coming around you than having to pass the slower ones. If you are a little unsure, still start further up in the group but keep to one side and take the inside line to the first buoy. If it is a deep water start give yourself lots of room, especially in front, so when the swimmer's feet in front of you come to surface you do not take a kick to the face. If it is a more traditional start at waist deep, dive in with a tight streamline and light to moderate kick, and if you can still touch the bottom with your hands, stand and dolphin dive until it is deep enough to swim.

FIRST 200

The first 200 yards (or metres) should include a strong first 50 that is not sprinting, but smooth and controlled, and you should be lightly kicking during this time. While the swimmers around you begin to slow, pick up your effort. Once you are up to speed, settle into your rhythm. If possible, avoid contact with other swimmers as it will slow you down. You should swim away from contact situations even if it feels like you are going off your line.

© Bakke-Svensson/Ironman

DRAFT LIKE A GENIUS

Once you have established your rhythm and position at 200 yards, start looking to draft another swimmer. Drafting in swimming is a perfectly legal strategy that can have big performance benefits – there can be up to 8 % energy savings while drafting another swimmer. Look for feet and bubbles and try to follow a slightly faster swimmer as close to their feet as possible without making contact.

PAY ATTENTION TO YOUR STROKE

Once in the draft take some time to review the technical aspects of your stroke. Start with your head. It is very common to keep your head high in the open water which will lead to an angled body position, tension in the neck, shoulders, and back, and ultimately an increase in drag with reduced efficiency. Keep your head low in the water! Place focus on rotating the hips – this will lead to a smooth rotation of the shoulders and a nice extension of the arms. When sighting, keep your chin in the water lifting your eyes just above the surface when your head is returning to the water after breathing.

LAST 200

When the shore is in sight and you are roughly 200 yards away, bring up the rate of your kick slightly to engage the legs. This will warm up the lower body muscles and joints providing more activation and circulation. Maintain your rhythm and think positive thoughts that will propel you through T1 and on to the bike and run. When your hands can touch the bottom, stand up and start running out of the water. Once your feet are out of the water, move your goggles to your forehead and leave your hands free to help you run until you arrive at your transition spot.

DON'T DWELL ON YOUR TIME

If you check your watch, and find your time slower than expected, don't fret about it. Swim course distances are often imprecise or conditions may have slowed everyone down. Don't start your bike depressed, wait until you see the results – you may have had a great swim despite what your watch says.

© Dan Smith

7   Bike Preparation

Cycling will account for the longest duration of time in your triathlon and provide an important bridge from the swim to the run. You should be comfortable on your bike, aerodynamic, and have a good plan for nutrition and hydration because this is where the majority of your intake will occur. Preparation in race week should consist of making sure your equipment is ready to go and that you are activated for you race.

RACE WEEK PREPARATION

Include the following items in your race week routine:

- Get your bike assembled as soon as you arrive – this will give you ample time to make adjustments or last minute repairs.

- When assembling your bike be sure to place adjustable items such as the seat, seat tube, head set, bars, and aerobars to the same position that you are accustomed to. Mark these well before you leave.

- Ensure everything is tight.

- Inflate your tires.

- Check your computer sensors.

- Visit the bike mechanics on site early in the week to get a quick tune up – don't save this for the day before the race.

- If flying, purchase CO_2 cartridges since you are not able to fly with these.

- Choose the wheels you will be racing on and practice with them before the race.

- Go for a light spin and when you get back, check the bike over once, especially that brake pads are not rubbing and everything is still tight and secure.

© SI Photography

© fotolia

KEY RACE WEEK WORKOUTS

During race week you should get in at least 2 rides. The first workout is designed for early to mid week and is shorter in duration but still include some efforts that simulate those of the race and will keep your body activated. This workout should be included mid week. The purpose of this workout is to:

- Rehearse pace sections and efforts for your race.

- Practice gearing and cadence you will use on race day.

- Provide fitness maintenance (maybe even a little fitness gain) with ample ability to recover and be ready for race day.

Warm-up:

30 minutes of easy spinning with 5 x 30 seconds accelerations

Main Set:

45 minutes of riding

Include 1 x 15 minutes at Race Pace

Recover with 15 minutes of easy spinning

1 x 10 minutes at Race Pace

Cool-down:

15-20 minutes of easy spinning

The second workout is designed for final activation. It should occur one or two days before the race. This workout will not rob any of your energy and will get you ready to race.

Warm-up:
10 minutes of easy spinning

Main Set:
10-15 minutes with 6 x 45 seconds accelerations up to race pace but with a slightly higher cadence (i.e. 95-100 RPM)

Cool-down:
5 minutes of easy spinning

BIKE STRATEGIES AND PACING

To prepare properly on race morning for a good bike performance, remember to fuel well, give yourself time for warm-up and complete your final bike checks. Once you have completed the swim and are on to the bike, follow these guidelines for your best bike.

© Bakke-Svensson/Ironman

SEGMENTING

Before the race, break down the bike course into smaller, manageable pieces, and create a goal for each. Use landmarks, turns in the course, mile markers, or whatever you want to divide the course up. This will not only make the bike go by faster, but it will allow you to revisit the goals that you want to achieve and keep your mind in the game. When racing, each time you reach the end of the segment, congratulate yourself then refocus on the next segment. This is a good strategy if you are having a rough day as well because it will keep you going!

BUILD INTO IT

Since the swim used primarily different muscle groups, it is important to allow the body and physiology to make the transfer to now use the cycling muscle groups. These muscles are the largest in the body and if they are stressed too hard from the start they will go anaerobic and produce lactic acid, a limiter in performance that will take time to metabolize. It is best to build in to the effort, focusing on breathing and gradually building your effort until you find a good rhythm and settle in at a level that you can maintain and will still allow you to run well off the bike.

GEARING AND CADENCE

Most triathletes will ride at a cadence that is too low and not change gears nearly as often as they should. Change gears often and try to anticipate what gear you will need for any upcoming changes in grade and switch early. Try to maintain a cadence of 90-95 RPM throughout the race – this is proven to be the fastest and most efficient cadence – it will help your run too!

PACING

Start out on the bike conservatively and ease into it. Ignore competitors that might be going harder than you are, and stick to your race plan. It has been shown that most triathletes, particularly men, maintain a very high effort for the entire ride, and put forth effort much higher than what they will be able to produce on the run. This leads to a strong bike performance but can result in a mediocre run performance and sub standard overall result. A heart rate monitor is a good tool to keep you consistent with your pacing.

© Dan Smith

8 Run Preparation

The run leg of the triathlon can be the most demanding, but if you are prepared, it can be considered the best part of a triathlon because:

- it's the final part with the finish line!

- there's barely any equipment to worry about.

- it's all about you, the athlete, in the purest form.

- it's the chance to see where your competitors are or simply cheer for others in the race.

- you can see your friends and family.

- it's where the race can be won or lost.

RACE WEEK PREPARATION

KNOW THE RUN COURSE AND THEN SEGMENT IT!

Seeing the run course in advance will help you be prepared. Start by reading the description posted on the race website in advance of the race, then once you arrive at the race, take an easy spin on the run course. Look for differences in grade, landmarks, and areas that may be exposed the elements. Use these elements to start segmenting the course. For example, if you were running the marathon at the end of an Ironman ask yourself what seems most attainable to you? Running one 26 mile run focusing on landmarks, or four 10 km runs, or maybe 26 one mile runs from aid station to aid station? Whatever you decide,

it's best to break your run into pieces and decide what you'd like to accomplish in each piece. If one section is hilly, plan to keep a strong, steady pace. If one section is particularly smooth, plan to pick up your pace by focusing on your turnover or focusing on closing a gap on a competitor ahead of you. Segmenting your run will help you focus on what needs to be done at that precise moment, not on how much more is left to go.

© Dan Smith

PREPARE MENTALLY

Because the run leg of the race is mentally exhausting, you should take time during the week to prepare your brain (see chapter 10). Visualize your run, think of past runs when you felt exceptionally good and focused. Go through the segments of the course and what goals that you can control. See yourself running well and being successful – especially across that finish line.

TAKE IT EASY

For tapering purposes, the last week before the race shouldn't include any long, vigorous runs, but rather 2-3 easy to moderate ones, ranging from 15 minutes to nothing greater than 45 minutes. The final week before your race is about resting and allowing your body to recover after weeks of training. The run has the most potential to fatigue in race week so keep it short so if in doubt – do less!

KEY RACE WEEK WORKOUTS

These workouts are designed to allow your body to recover and be rested for race day, but still provide great activation so you do not become lethargic and can perform at your race.

The purpose of the workouts is to:

* tune up where you will change speeds, focus on leg speed, and activate your physiology for race day.

* rehearse pace sections and efforts for your race.

* practice locking in your rhythm and technical cues for run form.

* provide fitness maintenance with ample ability to recover and be ready for race day.

FARTLEK RUN

Warm-up:

10 minutes of easy running

4 x 15 second Strides (accelerations) with 30s of recovery

Light Stretching

Main Set:

5 minutes of building tempo (very controlled – feel great)

6 x 90 seconds at slightly faster than race pace

90 seconds of easy, steady, running between each – hold good form

Cool-down:

10 minutes of easy running

As with the bike, the second workout is designed for final activation and should be planned for one or two days before the race.

Warm-up:

5 minutes of easy running

Main Set:

5 minutes with 5 x 30s picks up to race pace where you feel quick, light, and rhythmic

Cool-down:

5 minutes of easy running

© DMike Byrne

RUN STRATEGIES AND PACING

PACING

Similar to starting the bike, you should build into the run with a focus on cadence, form, and breathing. You will be switching to different muscle groups when you go on to the run so allow some time for this to happen. Try to be at your race effort by the first mile so that you don`t become accustomed to a slower pace and dial in your rhythm. You should be careful not to run too fast out of transition with the excitement of going on to the run and the crowds, yet you will need to focus on quick cadence with a shorter stride which can make you want to go a bit too fast at the start.

RUN FORM AND TECHNIQUE "HEAD TO TOE"

The following tips are great technical cues to think of as you are running:

Body

- All motion is linear – straight forward. Think light.

- Run tall with hips forward.

- Your head can be tilted down 3-5 degrees and eyes watch the horizon ahead.

- Shoulders should be relaxed and square, chest opened for breathing.

- Taking a deep breath can help you relax.

Feet

- Quick turnover (cadence).

- Shorter stride.

- Think "light" feet.

- Keep the foot strike landing directly under your body (not striding out in front).

Arms

- Arms set the rhythm.

- Quicker arms = quicker feet.

- Relaxed and keep shoulders low.

Hands

- Thumbs gently touch top of index fingers.

- Hands slights cupped, no clenching.

- Do not cross middle of chest.

- Hands travel "from pocket to chin" – you should be able to see the tops of your hands.

Things to Remember:

- A quicker cadence with a shorter stride will be much easier on your legs coming off the bike and will allow you to prevent fatigue and maintain rhythm.

- Keep moving and avoid walking.

- You can feel subjectively slow on the run but you can still be making good time.

- Have a number of technical running form cues prepared and ready to use.

- Use the aid stations.

- Thank the volunteers.

- Cheer on a fellow competitors, high-five a friend, fellow competitor, or volunteer and use the energy to drive forward.

- Remember that you are choosing to do this for the challenge so when it gets tough – embrace it! You are accomplishing something great.

- Look around and enjoy the day – Smile!

9 Transitions: The 4ᵗʰ Sport

Transitions are unique to triathlon and are often underestimated in terms of their importance. The value of efficient transitions is emphasized when scanning the results at the end of a race and realizing that many of your competitors were within mere seconds of each other. A smooth, fluid transition can set you up for a good ride or run and give you a better all around experience and result at the end of the day. If you don't want to spend the weeks after your race wondering "what if?" make sure you are well prepared for the best transition possible.

Remember, the greatest transitions are not necessarily the fastest but rather the most controlled. Efficiency and consistency are key factors as you will no doubt be managing a high heart rate as your muscle systems transfer from discipline to discipline. Attention to detail with transitions will allow you to fully utilize your training in the individual disciplines and give you the best overall result.

There are a few things to remember when preparing for transitions:

- Have a methodology for how you move from one discipline to the next, a clear order of actions.

- Keep transitions clean and simple.

- Know how to multi-task.

- Treat transitions as a sport in itself and include in your training.

- Visualize your transitions.

- Give yourself plenty of time to set up on race day.

TRANSITION STRATEGIES

PRACTICE

Treat transitions like the 4th discipline and include practice in your training routine. Set up a mock transition spot and lay out everything like you would at a race. After going for a swim or a ride, use this mock area to go through all the steps of your transition. Have a clear order of your actions and rehearse before you head out for your ride or run.

© Bakke-Svensson/Ironman

VISUALIZE

Mentally prepare by visualizing your transitions can be very effective. Know the order you want to complete your transition by writing it out from when you exit the swim to when you get on the bike and then again from the bike finish to the start of the run. Now close your eyes and see yourself performing these transitions and following the order that you want listed out. Be smooth and confident, not rushed.

ARRIVING AT THE RACE SITE

In some longer distance races the check in will take place the day before the race and depending on whether you are required to give transition bags with your gear, there may not be too much need for set up. If this is the case, it is still important to familiarize yourself with the transition entrance and exit and where your spot is located. If you are required to set up your transition on race day, get to the race venue early (at least 90 minutes before) to give yourself time to set up. In a scenario where you are permitted to choose a transition spot, select one that is as close to the bike exit as possible – it's much easier to run out of the transition area without having to transport your bike alongside you.

© Mark Creery

MARK YOUR TERRITORY

After finding your spot, mark it with something recognizable like a bright towel if allowed. This will help keep your spot clear and will deter other competitors from moving your bike or gear as they set up beside you. Place your towel on the side of the bike that you will run beside as you exit. Leave anything you'll need during the transition on top of the towel.

LAYOUT

Here are some quick tips on preparing your transition area:

* Rack your bike with the front wheel facing out (at the front) of your transition area by hooking the seat on the transition rack pole or placing the back wheel in the slot (ground racks).

* Position the bike so you have the most amount of space on the side that you will hold the bike when running out of the transition.

* Keep your shoes clipped on your bike (requires practice before the race) with elastics to hold them level with the ground.

* Place your helmet on your handle or aerobars. It should be upside down with the front of the helmet closest to you and chin straps out so you can simply flip it up and onto your head.

* Nutrition, water bottles, sunglasses, tools, flat kit, and anything else that you need should already be attached to your bike so the only item you need to put on is your helmet.

* If it is a cold day and you need to put on extra clothing, keep it easy to access by draping it over your bike.

* Run gear is on your towel at the back of your transition zone so that it is not kicked around by you or other competitors that are heading out on the bike or run.

* You may want to keep an extra water bottle at your transition for warm-up or a quick sip as you go on to the run.

© Bakke-Svensson/Ironman

DO A WALK-THROUGH

After your transition area is set up, landmark your area by identifying a tree, pole, or sign that is close to your spot and easy to see when exiting the water. Your bright towel will also help with this. After your swim warm-up, walk back to your spot in the same direction you will enter transition after the swim – it will look very different from when you walked away. This is also a good time to visualize your transition and mentally prepare.

AN EASY EXIT

Before the race, lube up your forearms and shins with cooking spray, Vaseline, or BodyGlide. For easier removal, you might even consider cutting the legs of your wetsuit, especially if it comes down to ankle level. While making your way to your transition area, unzip your wetsuit and pull it down to hip level. Take off your swim cap and goggles and have them in your hand.

KNOW YOUR CLOTHES

Trying to place clothing over your head onto a wet body with an extremely high heart rate and tired arms can be a sporting event in itself. Eliminate this by becoming comfortable cycling in your swimsuit or triathlon suit. If you must pull something over your head, make sure it doesn't bind easily when wet and consider using a tight fitting jacket or vest that can easily be zipped up. Lube or powder your bike and running shoes before the race for easy entry. Lube may also be necessary for your legs and crotch in longer races, so have it handy.

CHIN STRAPS

Triathletes struggle desperately with helmet chin straps. Make sure that your helmet has a strap with a clasp that will connect easily with cold and tired hands. Master buckling your helmet by practicing at home with your eyes closed. Remember that you must have your helmet done up before unracking your bike and that it should stay buckled until you have racked your bike at T2. Your helmet in transition should be the "first thing on, last thing off." Forgetting this rule can result in disqualification.

GET IN THE RIGHT GEAR OUT OF TRANSITION #1

Before you race, perform a last minute check to make sure your bike is ready! Check your tire pressure, brake clearance, that everything is tight, and ensure your water bottles are full. Your bike should be in a smaller easy gear—don't go for a bike warm-up in a big gear and forget to change it! You will pay the price when your bike feels like it weighs 1000 pounds. You want to start your ride with a high cadence.

BE READY FOR TRANSITION #2

Once you have racked your bike and removed your helmet, slip in to your running shoes, gather up your gear and head out! Often everything you need can be gathered up from your transition and put on while you run. Putting on your hat, fuel belt, and nutrition can be easily accomplished while running and can save you valuable seconds and help you keep momentum.

© Adrian Lamb

10 Mental Strategies

The mental game in endurance sport is a critical piece of the performance formula. Maximum performance is limited by physical condition, but it is a combination of both physical and mental skill that allows you to reach full potential. Confidence is the emotional state that almost always leads to a better result. We see this when an athlete, despite not being in their best fitness, returns to a race course where they have experienced success in the past and performs well again. Confidence is usually a product of preparation, goal setting, and then utilizing mental strategies on race day to stimulate and maintain a strong performance.

GOAL SETTING

Everyone sets goals for their triathlon whether they know it or not. Just signing up for the race and hoping to finish it are significant goals. More detailed goal setting can be very powerful because it will define your mental approach to preparation and competition. It motivates you to focus on what you want to accomplish, the steps you must follow to make it there, and ultimately a sense of achievement once you have reached the goal. The most effective goals are specific, realistic, and measurable. Before setting your goals you should take some time to look back on what you've done in the past. Review your race performances and training patterns, identify your strengths, weaknesses, and patterns of behaviors, and use this review as a foundation to develop your new goals. You should break your goals into two categories when listing them out: Process oriented goals and Outcome goals. A well structured plan will include both types of goals so that you not only set a clear accomplishment for your race (outcome), but you establish the way in which you will achieve your goal (process).

PROCESS GOALS

Often, triathletes fixate on measures of performance such as *"break 25 minutes in the swim"* or *"finish top 10 in my age group."* These performance standards are outcome goals that are not necessarily in the control of the athlete. Process goals are the actions the athlete will implement to try to achieve the desired outcome and are directly related to the athlete's behavior and philosophy. Process goals are small, detailed, and made up entirely of what you can control. Following process goals will often lead to a favorable outcome!

Examples of Process Goals

- Review my nutrition plan prior to the race.

- Commit to getting good sleep during race week.

- Enjoy the race experience.

- Keep a low head position in the swim.

- Sustain 90 RPM cadence on the bike.

- Follow my heart rate zones.

- Drink every 15 minutes.

- Celebrate with my family after the race.

OUTCOME GOALS

Focusing on outcome goals is in our competitive nature. Outcome goals are often the goals most discussed as they have a lot to do with time, speed, and placing. These goals are beneficial because it can help keep the athlete focused and motivated but there needs to be some degree of caution because they are sometimes out of the athlete's control and can lead to negative feelings despite a good performance. Outcome goals should be a good mixture of personal goals and competitive goals.

© Mike Byrne

Example of Outcome Goals:

- New personal best finishing time on a given course.

- Completing a distance you haven't tried before.

- New best time for one of the individual disciplines.

- Winning your age group.

- Beating a rival or training partner.

- Qualifying for a team.

- Qualifying for a World Championships race.

REVIEW YOUR GOALS AFTER THE RACE

Commit to your goals and work to make them a reality. A good way to achieve your goals is to the list them out in advance and tell someone about them. Goals are harder to go back on and therefore more likely to be achieved once they are out in the open. Use the week before your race to review and memorize your process goals. When you get a free moment, picture yourself reaching them, both the process and outcome. Once the race is completed, review your goal listing to reinforce the goals you achieved and review the ones you did not for future training and preparation.

POSITIVE SELF TALK

During the race you must execute your process goals in order to achieve your desired outcomes at the end of race. For most of the race you will be alone with your thoughts and that means that you will need to give direction to yourself and make decisions. This is called self talk and it is an incredibly powerful tool because not only will it allow you to take the focus off of the physical stress that your body is going through, it will provide a check on implementing your process goals. By reviewing your race process goals and by revisiting previous racing experiences prior to the race, you should be able to build an "inventory" of key messages that you can remind yourself of during the race. Self talk can be grouped into three categories: **technical**, **tactical** and **self encouragement**.

TECHNICAL STRATEGIES

Technical self talk should include cues that address sport-specific skills and whether they are being performed properly. If you have been given specific skills to focus on by a coach in training and you know this is effective for you, use it in your race. Focus on one technical skill and the cue that helps you perform the most efficiently. Try implementing the cue for 10 seconds (this will be a lot longer than you think).

This will accomplish 2 things; a nice distraction from the discomfort of your body working hard, and secondly if you are able to implement the skill well you will see an increase in efficiency or speed. A win-win! Remember to have these cues ready long before the race because it will be very difficult to come up with them in the middle of a race.

Examples of technical cues

Swim

"Low head, chin down"

"Light fast kick"

"Finger tips below my elbows after the catch"

Bike

"Spin – good cadence"

"Aero , low on my bike"

"Rhythm and breathing"

"Pulling up on the back of my pedal stroke"

Run

"Open up my chest and lungs"

"Short stride – cadence – quick light feet"

"High hands"

"Elbows tucked in"

TACTICAL STRATEGIES

Tactical self talk is not centered on skill but rather on tactical factors such as strategy, segmenting and pacing. Again, they are helpful in that they keep your head in the game for good decision-making and motivation, and also offer a distraction from the stress your body is going through. When an athlete comments that a race was "fun" it is often because they implemented and experienced many tactical strategies. The more prepared you are for these in advance of the race, the more "fun" you will have.

Examples of Tactical Cues

Swim

"Strong first 200 and then settle in"

"Get in a good draft off another swimmer"

"Work hard to the turn because I am swimming into the current and I will get a free ride back"

"Find a good rhythm between the 2 buoys"

"I'm going to swim for at least 40 strokes with the next athlete that passes me"

Bike

"Heart rate stays in zone 3"

"I'll check my pace at the next marker"

"After the next corner I will take in some calories"

"I am going to catch that next athlete up the road"

"I am going to build my effort each 10 miles on the bike"

"I am staying close to this athlete and not letting them get out of my sight"

Run

"Easy out of transition"

"Build and find my rhythm to the first mile marker"

"Where is my competition?

"This is 13 x 1 mile repeats"

"I will pick up my pace and see if I can hold it"

"Run 20 fast steps around every corner"

"Patience – save it for the second half"

"Run telephone post to telephone post"

"I'm going to run beside this person for five minutes to see what it's like"

"I know I can out-sprint that athlete"

SELF ENCOURAGEMENT

The third positive self talk strategy is self encouragement and it can be very powerful both mentally and physically. Encouragement will not only give confidence and raise spirits but will also release endorphins from the brain that will dampen signals of stress and pain from the body. A good rule is to say only things that your coach or a loved one would say and don't allow yourself to say anything that they would not. Your coach wouldn't say "you are too slow" or "your legs are heavy" so this means that you can't either. Chances are your supporters will shower you with positive comments and you should too. Self encouragement is all about self love and being prepared with the reasons why you are doing this.

Examples of Self Encouragement

"Keep pushing – you are strong"

"I'm proud of myself"

"I'm doing this for my family"

"Think of how good I will look after this race"

"Get to that finish line"

"I'm one of very few people in the world that can accomplish this"

"I'm on a mission!"

BREE WEE'S SELF ENCOURAGEMENT

It's not uncommon for triathletes to want to give up during a race, so self encouragement is the key when it gets down to the nitty gritty. Pro triathlete Bree Wee knows this well.

© Baron Sekiya

"During a race I'm constantly thinking . . . *I trained so hard, sacrificed a lot of time with family or friends, so I am going to work hard and have a great race*. I find that if I constantly think about all my hard work, I can usually push a little bit more."

Bree says that thinking of her son Kainoa is also a huge motivation.

"I always write Kainoa's name on my left hand and on my right running shoe. I look at my hand on my bike and find myself saying *"do this for little man."* When I'm running I look at my shoe and it reminds me to keep going, because its minutes I could be spending with him," Wee explains. "His name means "strong" in Hawaiian, so it always reminds me to stay strong."

Wee knows that self motivators can really help push through a race. By thinking of her son Kainoa and all of her hard work, Wee broke the all-time women's age group record in her first ever Ironman in Hawaii and earned podium finishes in both Ironman Japan and Ironman 70.3 in St. Croix.

HOW DO YOU MAKE POSITIVE SELF TALK WORK FOR YOU ON RACE DAY?

1. Know your process goals.

2. Be motivated by your outcome goals.

3. Visualize yourself achieving these goals.

4. List your technical, tactical, and self encouragement cues.

5. Rehearse these cues in practice.

6. Commit to at least 10 seconds of implementing each cue in the race.

7. At the end of the day celebrate what you've accomplished in the race, not what you haven't. If you do this you will "own" these successes and bring them along for your next races.

11 Race Taper Training Schedules

A race taper is structured by decreasing the training volume and frequency as you approach the race. Tapers can start anywhere from 4 weeks before a longer distance event to right up until the week of the race. A good taper will allow you to rebuild your glycogen stores for fueling the muscles, regenerate muscle tissue, and get optimum recovery. The general rule should be cutting back to 50 % of the volume and intensity, but not decreasing the level of intensity. The following are two different taper schedules that can be used when tapering for any distance of race. The weeks before this will vary more depending on the distance that you are racing. You will see some of the race week workouts demonstrated in earlier chapters incorporated into the schedules:

Sample Taper Schedule 1

Monday	Tuesday	Wednesday
Workout 1	**Workout 1**	**Workout 1**
Day Off	**Swim 1:00**	**Bike 1:30**
Full Day Off • Light Stretching • Possibly a light massage if available	Warm-up: • 300 free • 200 mixed stroke • 100 kick • 200 free breath every 5 strokes • 200 mixed stroke Main Set: 3 sets of: • 4 x 100 steady with 20s R (Recovery) • 100 choice stroke with 60s R • Each set gets faster Cool-down: 400 ez	Warm-up: • 30 min easy with 5 x 30s accelerations Main Set: • Include 1 x 15 min at Race Pace • 15 min Recovery • 1 x 10 min at Race Pace Cool-down: • 15-20min ez spin
	Workout 2	
	Run 1:00	
	Fartlek Run Warm-up: • 10min ez • 4 x 15s Strides with 30s R • Light Stretch Main Set: • 5 minutes of building tempo (very controlled – feel great) • 6 x 90s at slightly faster than race pace • 90s ez steady run between each – hold good form Cool-down: 10 min ez running	

Thursday	Friday	Saturday	Sunday
Workout 1	**Workout 1**	**Workout 1**	**Race Day**
Swim 1:00	**Day Off**	**Bike 0:30**	• Make time for race warm-ups.
Open Water	Full Day Off or an easy swim if desired	• Race Prep • 20-30 min ez spinning	Have a great race!
Warm-up: • 600 (10 min) • Practice race warm-up • Include 10 pick-ups (20 stokes fast/20 strokes easy)		• Include 4 x 60s pick-ups to race pace	
		Workout 2	
Main Set: • 1 x 300 (5 min) with 60s R steady • 1 x 500 (7 min) with 2min R at mid race pace • 1 x 300 (5 min) with 60 you're at your starting speed (strongest one)		**Swim 0:30**	
		• Open Water Race Prep • On race course if possible	
		• 10 min ez swimming and mixed stroke • 10 x 20 strokes fast/30 strokes ez • 3-5 min of loose easy swimming	
Cool-down: • 5 min easy			
Workout 2			
Run 0:30			
• 20-30 min ez run • Loosen legs • Include 2-3 light pick-ups for 30s			

Sample Taper Schedule 2

Monday	Tuesday	Wednesday
Workout 1	**Workout 1**	**Workout 1**
Day Off	**Swim 1:00**	**Bike 1:30**
Full Day Off • Light Stretching • Possibly a light massage if available	Warm-up: • 200 choice; • 12 x 75 (3 x free, Kick with no board, BK/BR/Free, Pull) Main Set: • 6 x 100 with 30s R at goal 1500 m • 100 m ez • 10 x 50 (20") alternating 50 m fast, 50 m easy. Cool-down: 200 non-free No other workouts today – This is the second day in a row with no bike or run to give legs excellent recovery	Warm-up: • 30 min including 5 min with RPM at 50 – low to moderate effort Main Set: • 2 x 10 min at race pace/effort with 10 min R Cool-down: • 20min easy with higher RPM **Workout 2** **Run 0:25** Brick Run Off the bike • 10 min at slightly below (slower) than race pace • 15 min ez

Thursday	Friday	Saturday	Sunday
Workout 1	**Workout 1**	**Workout 1**	**Race Day**
Swim 1:00	**Swim 0:30**	**Bike 0:30**	Make time for race warm-ups.
Warm-up: • 100 choice; • 3 x 300 (100 free, 100 IM, 100 Kick) Main Set: • 5-6 x 200 with 20s R Short rest, Steady aerobic. 1500 m pace + :03-:05/100m Cool-down: • 150 choice stroke • 3 x 50 Kick	• Race Prep • Open water Warm-up: • 100 choice Main Set: • 12 x 50 with 20s R alternating long distance per stroke and race pace • 4 x 50 with 20s R as 25 fast/25 ez Cool-down: • 5 min easy	Race Prep ride including 5 min at race pace. Test gears	Have a great race!
Workout 2		**Workout 2**	
Run 0:30		**Run 0:10**	
Warm-up: • 10 min easy running with a few light pick-ups Main Set: Fartlek: • 4 min steady, 2 min ez • 3 min at race pace, 2 min ez • 2 min slightly faster than race pace, 2 min ez • 1 min with good leg speed (not sprinting) with 5 min ez running		Light race prep run Warm up and stretch	
Workout 3			
Bike 0:30			
Optional 30 minute easy ride			

© Mark Creery

PowerBar

LifeSport

FINISHER
new balance
Victoria Triathlon

new balance
Victoria Triathlon

12   Post Race Recovery

Sometimes we are so motivated from a race, for the right reasons or not, that we yearn to begin training shortly after the race. The principle of supercompensation, in other words, our physiology adapting to become stronger, is based on overload and recovery. Without proper recovery there will not be supercompensation and you will miss an opportunity for performance gains.

To avoid the pitfalls of post-race training, it is important to plan a recovery strategy for each race. Develop a plan that will allow you to return to training with a fully recovered body, renewed energy and enthusiasm. Enhanced physical and mental recovery will catapult you to the next level and remember – the longer you go, the more you need to recover. Follow this guide to post-race recovery and when you should return to a full training schedule:

RECOVERY STRATEGIES

When can I start my full training program again?	
Sprint	1-2 days
Olympic	3-5 days
Half Ironman	7-10 days
Ironman	21-28 days

POST-RACE RECOVERY STARTS IMMEDIATELY

Recovery begins the moment you cross the finish line. The first priority should be hydration. Drink water or a fluid replacement drink as soon as possible at the conclusion of your event. Races usually provide apples, oranges, bananas, juice or other simple carbohydrate snacks to choose from. These foods will raise your blood sugar level and aid in quicker recovery.

Your post-race meal rich with complex carbohydrates should be ingested within 2 hours of the race finish. Your muscles are sponges for glycogen right after a race, so this meal is important to recover and gain energy that will help your training in the week following the event. The supercompensation has begun!

Massage is one of the oldest and best known methods of enhancing recovery. Get a massage after a race if you are already used to having them. If you are not used to it, a massage can create some unexpected muscle soreness. Ask the therapist to go gently if you are new to massage.

THE DAY AFTER

Write down how great it felt to achieve your goals. Take note of what you would do next time. Take all those inspiring thoughts and keep them in mind when training gets tough. Your body needs a rest even though your mind is ready to go out and conquer the world.

© Mark Creery

The day after your race should include several post-race recovery techniques. These may include a massage, hot-cold therapy, and a gentle workout to promote blood flow and muscle recovery.

Hot and cold therapy can be done in a variety of ways. Ideally, the athlete will immerse themselves for 90 seconds in water that is 12-13 degrees Celsius. Follow that with 3 minutes in the hot tub. The opening of arteries from the hot followed by assistance to the lymphatic system of the cold will stimulate blood flow and aid in regeneration. Complete this pattern 4 times during each hot/cold session.

If you can't resist a workout, a light spin on the bike of 20-30 minutes or a short swim will do the trick. Include plenty of non-free swimming to stretch and loosen fatigued muscles. A short swim set (i.e. 6x50 at 80-85 % of maximal heart rate on 60 sec.) will promote the clearance of waste products that were created during the race.

Your diet should still be focused on hydration and carbohydrate rich foods. You should also include protein in your meals to aid in the repair of muscle damage. The best mode of recovery is sleep. Try to make sure you are getting in at least 9-10 hours per night immediately following the race. If you have the luxury of taking a nap during the day, this will also help you to recover faster.

DAY 2 – A SURPRISE

Many athletes feel worse on the second day following a hard race. This is called Delayed Onset Muscular Soreness (DOMS). It can affect you 48-72 hours following an event. The best remedy for this soreness is movement.

This is a great day to head out on the bike. Keep the intensity low and spin (90-100 rpm on the flats) through the ride. Keep the duration of this ride to less than 75 minutes. You can include a short run of 15-20 minutes after this ride.

Running should be handled with care after a race. Carefully monitor the condition of your body and pay attention to any new aches or pains you may be experiencing. Sometimes a hard race can inflame old injuries or create muscle damage that, if left unchecked, could lead to injury if you go back to hard running too soon.

You can include some more massage and hot/cold therapy on day 2. This will speed the recovery process.

DAY 3-7 KEEP ACTIVE

Depending on the distance of the event, you will begin to reintroduce structured training but in the meantime keep active with activities that you may not normally do. This will also help provide variety and motivation. When you resume normal training, you must be careful not to increase the training load too quickly. Aim to return to your normal schedule but decrease training volume by 25-30 %. You can add some threshold or race pace, but avoid intense interval efforts and don't be afraid to cut workouts short and leave wanting more. Use your extra time to review your race, celebrate the goals that you achieved, and plan on how you will conquer the goals you didn't.

13 Coaching for Your Best Race

© Dan Smith

Having a great coach can really improve your opportunities for success. Triathlon can be all-encompassing so having an expert build your training program and support you with great advice generally leads to great success. If you have found the advice in this book valuable you may want to contact LifeSport for coaching. More information is available at:

www.lifesportcoaching.com

LifeSport Coaching is a proud to be the "Official Coaches of Ironman." LifeSport and Ironman have joined together to provide world-class coaching, training programs, and training camps for athletes competing in Ironman, 70.3 or shorter distance triathlons. LifeSport believes that excellent coaching should be available to anyone who has the desire to achieve their personal goals. Led by Olympic Gold Medal, 70.3 and Ironman coaches Lance Watson and Paul Regensburg, LifeSport offers personalized, systematic, and interactive training to athletes of all abilities.

At LifeSport our philosophy is based on providing customized training progressions while the athlete gains an education in both the sport and themselves. LifeSport training is structured to meet the athlete's goals by building a program that compliments the athlete's individual needs and lifestyle. With LifeSport coaches, there are no wasted workouts and no junk miles. LifeSport is proud to have coached numerous age group athletes to amazing accomplishments like completing their very first event, achieving personal records, and qualifying for Ironman World Championship Events. Our coaching interaction and personalized coaching programs emphasize fitness, performance and inspiration for all of our clients. The custom designed programs are guaranteed to help you achieve your goals and dreams.

Contact us and see how we can build the perfect program for you!

ABOUT THE AUTHOR

Paul Regensburg has served as a triathlon coach to athletes at Olympic, Commonwealth, and Pan American Games, and holds the highest possible level of coaching certification in triathlon – a National Coaching Institute Diploma and Triathlon Master Coach designation.

Regensburg has the distinction of guiding gold medal winning teams through a full cycle of major multisport games as the Triathlon Canada High Performance Director – a feat unmatched by any other Canadian sport. He has provided commentary for the Canadian Broadcasting Corporations Olympic Triathlon and founded the National Triathlon Center in Victoria, Canada where he was director and coach for five years.

Regensburg's coaching specialty lies in developing athletes to the internationally competitive level, and he has helped a number of athletes achieve their dreams of going to Olympic Games, World Championships, Ironman's, and other major events.

Currently residing in Victoria, Canada, Regensburg, along with Olympic Gold Medal Coach Lance Watson, heads LifeSport Coaching – an industry-leading coaching company designated as the Official Coaches of Ironman – where he works with amateur and professional athletes from around the world.

Additional Writing Credits: **Amee Nijjar**

PHOTO CREDITS

Cover photo: imago

Photos: see individual photos

Cover design: Sabine Groten

Ironman Edition
Ingrid Loos Miller
Weight Management For Triathletes

This guide provides practical information and tools that will help triathletes of all levels in their quest to improve body composition for performance and aesthetics while enjoying a multi-dimensional life. This book offers strategies for various eating styles, recognizing that men and women approach the issue differently. It describes the importance of low bodyfat for triathletes, how to use bodyfat data, implementing a weight control program over the long haul.

200 pages, full-color print
58 photos, 6 illustr., 16 charts
Paperback, 6^1/2" x 9^1/4"
ISBN 9781841262901
$ 18.95 US / $ 29.95 AUS
£ 14.95 UK / € 18.95

Ironman Edition
Cherie Gruenfeld
Become an Ironman

Become an Ironman is a treasure trove of deeply insightful training and racing wisdom. Its purpose is to provide the reader with a rich collection of insider tips, techniques and expertise.
Written in a straightforward, easily readable style, Become an Ironman is designed to deliver the most information in the fewest words possible. This guide is targeted at both shorter distance athletes and those who have already participated in an Ironman and want to improve their performance.

128 pages, full-color print
30 photos
Paperback, 6 ^{1}/2" x 9 ^{1}/4"
ISBN: 9781841261133
$ 16.95 US / $ 29.95 AUS
£ 12.95 UK / € 16.95

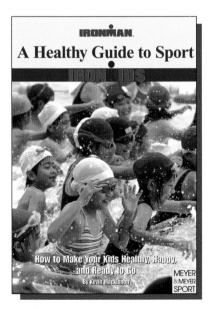

Ironman Edition: Ironkids
Kevin Mackinnon
A Healthy Guide to Sport
How to Make Your Kids Healthy, Happy, and Ready to Go

This book provides a comprehensive plan that helps parents guide their children towards a healthy love of sports. It will show parents and their kids how to get involved in triathlon and other "lifestyle" sports that can be pursued for a lifetime. A Healthy Guide to Sport will show you how sport can be the most enjoyable, healthy, and educational activity our children get to do.

128 pages, full-color print
48 photos, 12 illustrations
Paperback, 5^3/4" x 8^1/4"
ISBN: 9781841261065
$ 17.95 US / $ 29.95 AUS
£ 12.95 UK / € 16.95

Ironman Edition
Huddle/Frey/Babbitt
Starting out
Training for Your First Competition

Here's the best book on the market to get you to the starting line. Roch Frey and Paul Huddle are the two most respected names in multisport coaching. They cover all the basics in the first book of the Ironman Training Series. Besides running, cycling and swimming, you'll find information on everything from weight training to flexibility to nutrition. With Roch and Paul at your side, anyone and everyone can do a triathlon.

Ironman Edition
Ash/Warren
Lifelong Training
Advanced Training for Masters

Keen and ambitious masters who have already completed the Olympic/Short triathlon a number of times begin to strive for higher sporting achievements. The new challenge now is the Middle Distance and of course the 'magical' Ironman Distance. This book accompanies you in your entire training preparations as well as through competition.

For more books on triathlon visit
www.m-m-sports.com

■ **E-Mail**
sales@m-m-sports.com

■ **online**
www.m-m-sports.com

■ **Telephone / Fax**
+49 2 41 - 9 58 10 - 13
+49 2 41 - 9 58 10 - 10

■ **Mail**
MEYER & MEYER Verlag
Von-Coels-Str. 390
52080 Aachen
Germany